TRANSFORMATIONAL CHANGE IN
COMMUNITY COLLEGES

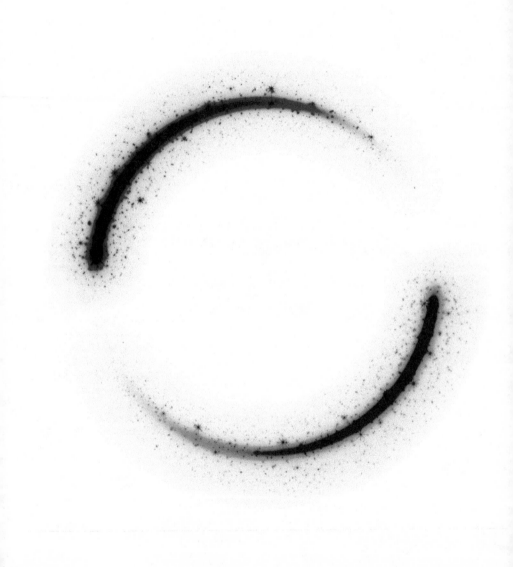

TRANSFORMATIONAL CHANGE IN COMMUNITY COLLEGES

Becoming an Equity-Centered Institution

Christine Johnson McPhail and Kimberly Beatty

Foreword by Walter G. Bumphus

STERLING, VIRGINIA

COPYRIGHT © 2021 BY STYLUS PUBLISHING, LLC

Published by Stylus Publishing, LLC
22883 Quicksilver Drive
Sterling, Virginia 20166-2019

Library of Congress Cataloging-in-Publication Data
Names: McPhail, Christine Johnson, author. | Beatty, Kimberly, author.
Title: Transformational change in community colleges : becoming an equity-centered higher education institution / Christine Johnson McPhail and Kimberly Beatty ; foreword by Walter G. Bumphus.
Description: First edition. | Sterling, Virginia : Stylus Publishing, LLC., 2021. | Includes bibliographical references and index. |
Identifiers: LCCN 2021007554 (print) | LCCN 2021007555 (ebook) | ISBN 9781620369661 (cloth) | ISBN 9781620369678 (paperback) | ISBN 9781620369685 (adobe pdf) | ISBN 9781620369692 (epub)
Subjects: LCSH: Community colleges--United States--Administration. | Education, Higher--Aims and objectives--United States. | Educational equalization--United States. | Educational change--United States.
Classification: LCC LB2341 .M3664 2021 (print) | LCC LB2341 (ebook) | DDC 378.1/01--dc23
LC record available at https://lccn.loc.gov/2021007554
LC ebook record available at https://lccn.loc.gov/2021007555

13-digit ISBN: 978-1-62036-966-1 (cloth)
13-digit ISBN: 978-1-62036-967-8 (paperback)
13-digit ISBN: 978-1-62036-968-5 (library networkable e-edition)
13-digit ISBN: 978-1-62036-969-2 (consumer e-edition)

Printed in the United States of America

All first editions printed on acid-free paper
that meets the American National Standards Institute
Z39-48 Standard.

Bulk Purchases
Quantity discounts are available for use in workshops and for staff development.
Call 1-800-232-0223

First Edition, 2021

This text is dedicated to all students, especially those of color, in America's community colleges who will benefit from the transformational change that leads to an equitable approach to their preparation, learning, and achievement.

CONTENTS

FOREWORD
Walter G. Bumphus ix

PREFACE xi

ACKNOWLEDGMENTS xv

1 CREATE A CULTURE FOR TRANSFORMATIONAL CHANGE
THROUGH AN EQUITY LENS 1

2 CREATE A SENSE OF URGENCY FOR EQUITY THROUGH
THE EXISTING ORGANIZATIONAL CULTURE 14

3 IDENTIFY AN EQUITY COALITION THROUGH GOVERNANCE
AND BY MOBILIZING OTHERS 27

4 FORM A STRATEGIC EQUITY VISION THROUGH
GOVERNANCE WITH CLEAR COMMUNICATION AND
INTENTIONAL COLLABORATION 37

5 COMMUNICATE THE EQUITY VISION THROUGH
INTENTIONAL COLLABORATION AND THE
GOVERNANCE PROCESS 42

6 UTILIZE INSTITUTIONAL LEADERSHIP AND
COLLABORATION TO EMPOWER EMPLOYEES INTO
BROAD-BASED ACTION 55

7 GENERATE SHORT-TERM WINS THROUGH RELATIONSHIP
CULTIVATION 63

8 CONSOLIDATE GAINS UTILIZING INSTITUTIONAL LEADERSHIP 71

9 ANCHOR EQUITY INTO THE CULTURE THROUGH
GOVERNANCE AND REVAMPING THE INSTITUTIONAL
INFRASTRUCTURE 82

10 PROMOTE EQUITY IN THE FIELD 87

11 FOCUS ON EQUITY IN ACTION 104

12 LAUNCH THE CALL TO ACTION: WHAT DOES AN
EQUITY-CENTERED INSTITUTION LOOK LIKE? 114

REFERENCES 119

APPENDIX A: INSTITUTIONAL SELF-ASSESSMENT FOR EQUITY 123

APPENDIX B: KOTTER'S (2004) LEADING CHANGE MODEL 129

APPENDIX C: AACC (2018) LEADERSHIP COMPETENCIES 130

ABOUT THE AUTHORS 131

INDEX 133

FOREWORD

Redesign. Reinvent. Reset: Becoming an Equity-Centered Institution

In the past couple of decades, hundreds of community college leaders throughout the United States have launched efforts aimed at improving equity in student outcomes. Challenged by external changes in demographics, technology, enrollments, fiscal support, federal and state mandates, and outdated programs, many leaders are struggling to find ways to implement their equity agendas. Unfortunately, the hundreds of efforts to improve equitable outcomes have had mixed results. While many institutions can demonstrate that some changes produced equitable outcomes for some students, *few* institutions have made dramatic transformational changes.

Further, some institutions report that they have only been able to make essential changes in parts of their operations such as offering programs for specialized populations and encouraging faculty to use different pedagogical practices. Although many community colleges have used "democracy's colleges" as their moniker, too many community colleges are still struggling or have lost their courage to promote scalable equity efforts. Exactly why some community colleges have launched successful equity agendas and others have not is unclear. And, community college scholars have not fully studied the many equity efforts that are taking place at the nation's community colleges.

McPhail and Beatty's book is a valiant effort to provide higher education with a strategic approach to implementing an equity agenda. The authors— a former community college president and university professor and a current community college chancellor—look at the implementation of the equity agenda through the use of Kotter's eight-step change model and the American Association of Community College's (AACC) competencies for community college leaders. They offer both theoretical and practical leadership approaches to embed equity into the culture of the institution. The authors skillfully guide the reader through the change process and vividly describe the leadership competencies required to move the equity agenda to the next step. They recommend maximum engagement among different stakeholders while urging bold and courageous direction from senior leadership teams. McPhail and Beatty admit that *change* and *equity* in a higher education institution are complex and challenging. Both McPhail and Beatty have walked in the shoes of faculty, led and managed change efforts, watched the change process unfold at other institutions, and studied how the equity agenda has progressed at many institutions. In this book, they share what they have learned.

The authors offer suggestions on how institutions can launch and sustain an equity agenda. Their recommendations are not cast in stone, and they are aware that there is no such thing as a one-size-fits-all proposition for initiating and sustaining equity. The book provides insights and direction.

Transformational Change in Community Colleges is a significant contribution to the ongoing struggle to find practical approaches to implementing an equity agenda in higher education. While many of the books on equity are informative about the topic, they are not very helpful when it comes to leading and implementing equity as a change process. Becoming an equity-centered institution requires leaders to redesign, reinvent, and reset their approaches to implementing the equity agenda. This book is a way to jumpstart these strategies.

American colleges and universities cannot escape the imperatives of equity in higher education. This book provides valuable information that leaders can use to institutionalize the equity imperative. The authors understand that equity-centered change efforts are still under development at many institutions. Institutions are at different stages in the implementation process, as demonstrated by the Achieving the Dream's national perspectives and from the three institutions featured in the book (the Colorado Community College System, Kellogg Community College, and Metropolitan Community College). McPhail and Beatty have used their wide-ranging knowledge and expertise to frame a new way of looking at implementing the equity agenda— the change process—from which the higher education community can learn how to become an equity-centered institution.

Walter G. Bumphus
President and CEO
American Association of Community Colleges

In order to understand what it means to be an equity-centered institution, practitioners must develop a foundational knowledge of equity principles, an understanding of the key transformational change elements critical to achieving equity, and the leadership competencies necessary to execute change. We wrote this book to provide a framework for learning these necessary skills in a way that emphasizes equity as a core value of the institution and as a role of leadership in promoting and sustaining equity-centered institutions. Becoming an equity-centered institution starts with building awareness and committed leadership at all levels of the institution. This text emphasizes the necessary requirements for building and maintaining these skills in order to make decisions and execute equity-centered strategies—that is the essence of becoming an equity-centered institution.

When we look at the dynamics of equity in higher education, it is easy to see why equity can be a challenging topic to teach, learn, and execute. Awareness and experience in equity-centered environments are what higher education practitioners need, yet this takes time. Until practitioners get this experience, it is up to senior leadership teams to provide them with an equity-centered conceptual framework and introduce them to the skills necessary for understanding and implementing successful equity-centered programs and services. This text will help accomplish these teaching and leadership development challenges.

Goals

We had three main goals in writing this text:

- **Relevance**: This book is the result of many years of teaching, leading, researching, and coaching individuals and institutions about equity inside higher education. It is important to teach our stakeholders skills that are based on research from the fields of education, leadership, and organizational change. We believe we accomplish this through the integration of AACC's leadership competencies for community college leaders into the equity conversation. Despite targeting community college educators with the leadership competencies, the competencies are applicable for all higher education practitioners. This book places a clear emphasis on awareness and teaching skills first but also ensures that those skills are based on practical application in the field.

- **Practical application**: To describe and explain equity and transformational change concepts, this book provides step-by-step implementation approaches that can be used to integrate equity-centered principles into practices and policies to implement or improve equity work into the organizational culture.

- **A purposeful approach**: We defined the act of becoming an equity-centered institution in terms of a transformational change approach using Kotter's eight-stage process. Kotter's eight-stage change model and AACC's leadership competencies for community college leaders are introduced in chapter 1 and integrated throughout the book. This integrated framework allows practitioners to place the intersectionality of equity, transformational change, and requisite leadership competencies into the larger context of higher education. While we used Kotter's eight-step change model, we emphasize that operations and situations inside higher educational institutions are not linear as implied in it. We show how the stages of change may occur at different times and in different situations at different institutions. We demonstrate what leadership competencies are recommended for each stage in the change process.

Our Strategy

The title of this book, *Transformational Change in Community Colleges: Becoming an Equity-Centered Institution*, points to two fundamental components of leadership—leading change and leadership competencies. With the exception of the first chapter where the foundation is set, chapter highlights and leadership competencies that are required for each phase of the transformation process will be provided.

The text also provides readers with information to discover the unique dynamics of transformational change, the essential competencies to lead change, and processes that pave the way to successfully launch initiatives to become an equity-centered institution. By examining processes through each of these lenses, readers come to understand the dynamic interplay of each and learn to treat each concept as a unique component of transformational change. To be competent in implementing transformative change such as equity, as this text emphasizes, readers must learn to identify each equity situation as unique, assess what competencies are needed to execute it, and effectively apply the appropriate skills and procedures at the right time in the right situation. In essence, the goal of this text is to provide a toolbox from which practitioners can draw in any equity situation—whether developing a committee on campus or hiring a new employee. To initiate this process, practitioners must first become aware of the needs of the institution, their own leadership competencies, and the ways in which they can be used to build and sustain equity-centered institutions.

ACKNOWLEDGMENTS

Developing our ideas about equity-centered intuitions and turning them into a book was as hard as it sounds. However, our experiences have been both challenging and rewarding. We especially want to thank the individuals that helped make this happen.

This book wouldn't have been possible without our many friends and colleagues—at higher education institutions throughout the nation—who allowed us to develop and test insight-related ideas in projects, workshops, and consulting engagements over the last 10-plus years. We owe a deep debt of gratitude to those who shared thoughts and provided constructive feedback on our work.

We want to acknowledge Ryan Ross, associate vice chancellor for Student Affairs, Equity, and Inclusion at the Colorado Community College System; Karen Stout, president and CEO of Achieving the Dream, Inc.; and Jorge Zaballos, chief equity and inclusion officer and their colleagues at the respective institutions for their contributions to the book in chapter 10: "Promote Equity in the Field." Their contributions reflect how community college leaders are always eager to test new ideas, new ways of thinking, and new practices to serve students.

We are grateful for the work that came before us that informed our thinking about this subject: Kotter's phenomenal approach to leading change that was adapted to leading in community colleges. Also, the AACC's development of the leadership competencies informs *how* leaders navigate the change toward becoming an equity-centered institution. We also acknowledge the work of the New England Resource Center for Higher Education (NERCHE). We used an adapted version of NERCHE's Self-Assessment Rubric for the Institutionalization of Diversity, Equity, and Inclusion in Higher Education to collect feedback from practitioners in the field about the equity work that is taking place at their institutions.

We are deeply indebted to Melissa Giese, executive director of Institutional Research at Metropolitan Community College, who assisted with the design and administration of the questionnaire. We can't thank her enough for being an unrelenting source of support for our efforts.

Particular words of appreciation go out to David Brightman, senior editor, Higher Education, Stylus Publishing. We sincerely appreciate his enthusiastic response to our book proposal and support throughout the book's developmental stages.

Finally, we want to extend special thanks to our husbands, Kelvin Beatty and Irving Pressley McPhail, for their support and tolerance of our numerous disappearances while working on the book. They always inspired and encouraged us to get this book finished!

CREATE A CULTURE FOR TRANSFORMATIONAL CHANGE THROUGH AN EQUITY LENS

Chapter highlights: In this chapter, we create a foundational understanding of equity and the framework for transformational change in becoming an equity-centered institution is introduced.

There is a growing recognition of the importance of equity in higher education in the United States. Public higher education has encountered rising inequality and inequities, which are, in turn, partly responsible for the equity disparities we see in our institutions through student achievement gaps, programmatic and support services, and employee recruitment and retention.

Ready or not, diversity, equity, and inclusion issues have stepped inside the open door of the American community college. Hailed as democracy's college, American community colleges are often regarded as the best in the world. However, recent community college reform initiatives (Achieving the Dream, Completion by Design, and Developmental Education Initiatives) implicitly suggest that the system could be much better if programs were in place to support and nurture a culture that hinges on programs and policies that support students of color and a culture of diversity, equity, and inclusion. Community colleges are a microcosm of their larger communities, and they can be a focal point to address larger societal issues. Equity must be positioned in the front and center of the issues facing community colleges. As protests over racial tensions continue to capture the nation's attention, it is increasingly important for community college leaders to pay deeper attention to what is taking place at the doors of and inside their institutions.

Although the majority of Black and Hispanic undergraduate students in the United States study at community colleges, Bill Moore (2006), a professor in the Community College Leadership Program at The University of Texas at Austin, declared his belief that discrimination was alive and well in community colleges. Moore believed that community colleges still operated in a "good-old boy" system, arguing that race is a difference that makes a difference. We agree with Moore and suggest that an equity-centered teaching and learning environment can be the difference that changes the game for underserved student populations in community colleges. While there is no recent research that discounts Moore's 2006 arguments, some institutions have acknowledged achievement disparities and are now moving toward an understanding of equity as well as equality.

John Brooks Slaughter (2003), the first African American director of the National Science Foundation and a distinguished academic leader, suggested that American higher education is a microcosm of American society. He argued that American higher education is an evolution that must be guided and nurtured by those who understand the essential role that American colleges and universities play in improving our society.

The persistence of educational disparities in the community college sector makes the concept of equity urgently important, and equity conversations must be guided by those who understand the role of community college leaders at every layer of the institution. If community colleges are to be relevant to all students, equity values must be embedded in the culture, mission, and overall fabric of the college.

No longer can community college educators hide behind historic open-door admission policies, suggesting that open access policies alone are sufficient to provide for the educational needs of *all* students. Today's community college leaders must embrace equity in all aspects of their leadership. Community colleges can no longer be about only access and opportunity; today's college leaders must examine how their students and employees are *treated* and what support structures are in place to accommodate their needs in order to improve success rates, retention, and close achievement gaps. In 21st-century institutions, management of issues related to equity is an urgent leadership imperative.

While equity in higher education may increasingly be respected as a fundamental characteristic, many community colleges have yet to link equity to the core values of the institution. Colleges can demonstrate *equity-centeredness* by engaging people from diverse backgrounds, treating them fairly, and including their perspectives in the way the college conducts its business. According to Bensimon (2005), the term *equity-mindedness* refers to the perspective or mode of thinking exhibited by practitioners who call attention to patterns of inequity in student outcomes. More and more community college leaders are adding equity to their strategic plans, and it's long overdue. Outdated policies and practices prevent colleges from realizing the full potential of a diverse and inclusive institution—equity is the first domino in the plan for colleges to become diverse and inclusive institutions. Too many organizations are still focused only on counting the numbers (race); others are focused on the events (inclusion); yet until organizations focus on the core issue—equity—organizational cultures will not change.

Some higher education leaders pay lip service to equity and may not necessarily have institutionalized the policies and procedures to make these values real. Equity is more than measuring student and employee demographics and support for a few special programs and services. As the local communities served by community colleges have changed, the new populations of students and employees must carefully evaluate how the institution relates to them. If community colleges do not connect with them in a relevant manner, they will begin to question the institution's authenticity and relevancy.

The higher education leaders who are bold enough to embrace equity as an institutional core value will reap enormous benefits in an improved institutional climate and with the success of students. When equity is practiced at the college, stakeholders' behavior demonstrates engagement and support for the mission. A diverse and inclusive environment enables all stakeholders to contribute their full potential in pursuit of the college's goals. The equity-friendly environment involves the celebration of various cultures, religions, and ethnicities. Colleges can sponsor cultural competence educational opportunities that provide students, faculty, and staff with skills and knowledge to become global citizens. But, let's keep it real—equity is not an event. It is a fundamental core institutional value, and it is imperative that community colleges employ policies and practices that embrace and support diversity, equity, and inclusion as core values (American Association of Community Colleges, 2014).

Launching an equity agenda may inspire both positive and negative responses at a college. However, connecting with underserved populations requires institutions to alter their policies and practices. We argue that equity efforts also require the institutions to push for behavioral changes from its employees. Getting entrenched administrators, faculty, and staff to change is difficult. For some leaders, implementing programs to promote equity may bring about added concerns to an already full plate of competing programs and leadership challenges.

Some entrenched educators may dismiss newly launched equity efforts because they have witnessed the development of numerous other special initiatives that did not go anywhere. They might see the equity agenda as just another passing fad. Further, in some cases faculty and administrators may view equity efforts as a path to lower academic standards in order to accommodate disadvantaged students. One of the first concerns that some leaders express when considering the prospect of adding an equity focus to the college's agenda or strategic plan is fitting additional programs into an already underfunded environment. Unfortunately, many well-meaning equity initiatives fail because organizations push them only as a compliance issue. In other situations, equity-oriented programs are established as appendage programs that are never mentioned in the college's strategic plan. Some institutions seek to develop college-wide programs to increase equity without necessary input and buy-in from stakeholders.

Leaders of public higher education institutions have decisions to make regarding the types of changes to make in order to institutionalize equity. The changes that higher education institutions will need to make can be based on the core values of their local institution (Alfred et al., 2009; Kim & Mauborngne, 2005). However, we acknowledge that institutional change is embedded in a network of influence and power from a variety of sources. Leaders cannot assume all sources will agree that equity-minded policies and practices are necessary. Leadership in this context calls for an effective analysis of resistance to equity and the barriers that need to be removed. What are the barriers, and where do they come from? Resistance to change can be viewed as the act of opposing or struggling with modifications or transformations that alter the status quo in the workplace (Kotter, 1996). Resistance to change can emerge from internal and external sources.

It is generally understood that managing resistance to change is challenging. Burke (2008) argued that organizations are striving to succeed in an increasingly complex global, political, and economic environment. He noted that organizations can experience different types of change. In our work, we have observed that resistance to change does not come in a single form. Change can emerge from groups and individuals within the institution, as well as from external groups. It can be covert or overt, organized or individual. In some instances, resistance emerges when there is a threat to something the individual values. For example, Evans (1996) discussed the human side of change. The author noted that real-life resistance may arise from a genuine understanding of the change or from a misunderstanding of the issues. Failure to adequately consider the complexity of the resistance can compromise the implementation.

Complex structures, policies, and processes can make it difficult to anchor equity into the organization's culture. An organization can break this barrier by employing diligent, quality, and highly effective leaders to navigate the terrain. It is important to have leaders who understand the culture of the organization. When organizational changes such as equity programs are forced on the institution, stakeholders are likely to push back. When pushback or resistance happens, the best approach for leaders of change is to understand the reasons for the resistance and then strive to strategize around those issues.

The pushback is likely to occur because leaders do not take the time to assess the current state of their organization. Trying to introduce and implement an equity agenda without conducting an assessment and understanding the current blueprint of the organization is a common behavior in many organizations that prevents progress.

As community colleges take on the equity challenge in efforts to transform their institutions, they must understand the concept of equity, the institution's culture, and committed leadership to accomplish the task. In some cases, the institution's culture can be the strongest barrier to progress; however, by beginning with the end in mind, coupled with dedicated leadership, the cultural tide can change, but it will take time.

Frequently, higher education leaders suggest that they want to implement equity because they have the belief that equity-centered policies and practices will bring significant change to the institution as a whole. However, we argue that the primary objective for institutionalizing equity is that the change will improve the environment of the organization on a daily basis.

Framework for Leading the Equity Challenge

For the purpose of this discussion, we intend for *leadership* to refer to a board of trustees or regents, an executive leadership team, governance leaders (faculty and staff), and other leadership positions as defined by the individual college. For the purpose of developing a culture of equity that leads to institutional change, leadership refers to any person or group that can influence and mobilize the institution toward the desired outcome. The desired outcome in this case is for institutions to create an equity-minded student and an employee experience that leads to success, completion, and retention for students and employees. For many institutions, this will be a heavy lift! That's why it is incumbent on the leadership team to set the tone for access and equity and make it a priority for the institution. Throughout the book, we integrated three concepts for institutions to use to become equity-centered institutions: (a) common definition of equity (Bensimon, 2005); change model (Kotter, 1996); leadership competencies (AACC, 2018).

Equity Lens Defined

In today's society, and particularly in higher education, the term *equity* is often misunderstood and associated within the context of racial equality. It is essential that the college community understands the difference between equity and equality. Equity in higher education, according to Bensimon (2005), refers to access to and success in higher education among historically underrepresented student populations. The focus of these types of equity conversations are topics such as ethnic minority and low-income students.

Bensimon (2005) defines three components of equity: (a) representational equity, which refers to the proportional participation of historically underrepresented student populations at all levels of an institution; (b) resource equity, which takes into account the proportion of educational resources that are directed at closing equity gaps; and (c) equity mindedness, which refers to the priority that the institution gives to equity efforts. The concept of equity requires institutional leaders and staff to demonstrate both awareness and a willingness to address differences by instituting policies and practices to serve all students. Equality, on the other hand, refers to giving people the same opportunity.

It is generally believed that everyone has the same access to community colleges. However, it is unrealistic to assume that everyone is starting at the same point or that all experiences that people bring to the educational experience are the same. As practitioners, we know that is not the case.

Community colleges were built on the idea of access. In essence, all students have the "same" access to higher education, learning resources, and faculty (Cohen et al., 2014). To examine this thought deeper, community college employees are hired using the "same" processes and experience their jobs the "same" as everyone else, therefore experiencing the institution the "same" as everyone else. The "sameness" minimally meets the true meaning of access as intended when we think of the community colleges as the lever that democratized higher education. Yes, community colleges provide equal access for all who want to learn and work in this great institution, but what happens once they are employed or admitted and equity enters the picture?

Equitable practices recognize that everyone who works or learns at the college has different experiences that may require different approaches to working and learning. Equity ensures that all students and employees can fairly and successfully participate in the institution's programs and services.

It is important to demonstrate that there are different levels of equity associated with the goal of becoming an equity-centered institution. Leaders are encouraged to develop a plan to become an equity-centered institution. It is likely that many higher education administrators and faculty have made clear distinctions between the terms *equality* and *equity*. Since most colleges and universities have clearly defined entry requirements, some practitioners likely believe that access is not an issue. Throughout this text, access is integrated into the discussion primarily because access is one of the first steps to enter college; when colleges transition to equity-minded institutions, they routinely examine all policies, procedures, and practices dealing with access and progression through college.

When we view the college experience through the equity lens, we operate from the position of fairness (see Figure 1.1). In essence, we design processes and strategies that address historical barriers so that everyone starts with the same tools. In using this approach, equity leads to greater success when considering the student and employee experience.

Figure 1.1. Equality versus equity.

EQUALITY

EQUITY

We can't get to "equal" when we have unaddressed historic deficits.

EQUALITY = SAMENESS
Giving everyone the same
thing = it only works if everyone
starts from the same place.

EQUITY = FAIRNESS
Access to same opportunities =
We must first ensure equity
before we can enjoy equality.

Now, let's talk about the "lens." The purpose of this text is to provide a guide for institutions to strive toward becoming an equity-centered institution—this is where "the lens" comes into play. Once an institution is committed to the process of leading this type of transformational change, all processes, programs, and infrastructures will be designed with equity at the forefront of the transformation. The equity lens requires an understanding of the meaning of equity; as Bensimon (2005) said, it is becoming "equity minded." Equity is the launching point for transformational change. We argue that community college leaders must demonstrate the leadership competencies to lead this change.

Overview of Kotter's 8 Step Process for Leading Change

From experience in the field we have observed that for change to be successful, there must be a strong commitment from the senior leadership team. We also note that stakeholders must recognize the need for change and to some extent determine a sense of urgency to launch a change effort. Moreover, we do not know any institutions that have launched successful change processes without addressing these challenges. We know that there are many community college leaders throughout the United States struggling to find ways to implement their equity agendas. Unfortunately, many of these efforts fail or at best fall short of their original goals because the institution's leadership team either lacks the competencies to lead the change, show little interest in the proposed change effort, or fail to have a plan to guide the change. We selected Kotter's (1996) eight-step change model for our work because the model addressed the issues that we believe to be important to effective in implementing a transformational change process. Kotter's (1996) eight-step change model consists of the following principles:

1. Create a sense of urgency: Create the catalyst for change.
2. Build a guiding coalition: Assemble a group with enough power to lead the change effort.
3. Create a vision for change: Create a vision to help direct the change effort.
4. Communicate the vision: Use every channel and vehicle of communication possible to communicate the new vision and strategies.
5. Remove barriers: Remove obstacles to change.
6. Create short-term wins: Recognize and reward employees involved in these improvements.
7. Consolidate improvements: Reinvigorate the processes with new projects, themes, and change agents.
8. Institute the change: Create the connections between new behaviors and corporate successes.

Overview of AACC's Leadership Competencies for Community College Leaders

The AACC (2018) leadership competencies for community college leaders reflect the skills necessary to be a leader advancing a student success agenda or a member of a team actively engaged in implementing student success initiatives and activities. The competencies are described as follows:

1. **Organizational culture**: An effective community college leader embraces the mission, vision, and values of the community college and acknowledges the significance of the institution's past while charting a path for its future.
2. **Governance, institutional policy, and legislation**: An effective leader is knowledgeable about the institution's governance framework and the policies that guide its operation.
3. **Student success**: An effective leader supports student success across the institution and embraces opportunities to improve access, retention, and success.
4. **Institutional leadership**: An effective leader understands the importance of interpersonal relationships, personal philosophy, and management skills in creating a student-centered institution.
5. **Institutional infrastructure**: An effective community college leader is fluent in the management of the foundational aspects of the institution, including the establishment of a strategic plan, financial and facilities management, accreditation, and technology master planning.
6. **Information and analytics**: An effective community college leader understands how to use data in ways that give a holistic representation of the institution's performance and is open to the fact that data might reveal unexpected or previously unknown trends or issues.
7. **Advocacy and mobilizing/motivating others**: An effective community college leader understands and embraces the importance of championing community college ideals, understands how to mobilize stakeholders to take action on behalf of the college, and understands how to use all of the communications resources available to connect with the college community.
8. **Fundraising and relationship cultivation**: An effective community college leader cultivates relationships across sectors that support the institution and advance the community college agenda.
9. **Communication**: An effective community college leader demonstrates strong communication skills, leads, and fully embraces the role of community college spokesperson.

10. **Collaboration**: An effective community college leader develops and maintains responsive, cooperative, mutually beneficial, and ethical internal and external relationships that nurture diversity, promote the success of the college community, and sustain the community college mission.

11. **Personal traits and abilities**: An effective leader possesses certain personal traits and adopts a focus on honing abilities that promote the community college agenda.

The equity-centered transformational change framework (Figure 1.2) illustrates how the three concepts interplay to to transform an institution toward becoming equity centered. While all three of the concepts are important, we argue that the driving force for change to be effective is committed

Figure 1.2. Equity-centered transformational change framework.

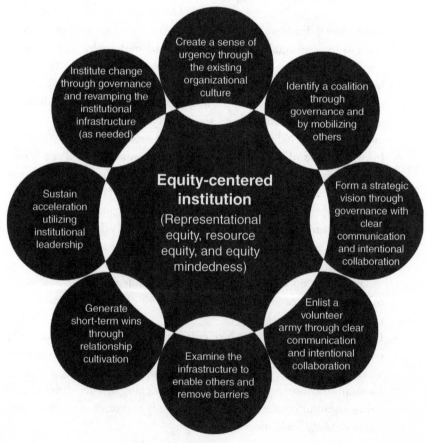

leadership. A commitment from the leadership team is essential to help stakeholders understand equity and transform the institution.

Figure 1.2 shows the key features of the equity-centered transformational change framework that will be explored in-depth in the following section:

Create a sense of urgency through the existing organizational culture. Since equity may be a "new" concept to some institutions, leaders must first scan the institution's culture to assess existing policies and practices. Leaders must engage the internal and external stakeholders to better understand institutional values/norms that may become a barrier to developing an equity-centered culture. An organizational culture scan can be a reality check for an institution. However, scanning the culture or environment is an essential step in the change process. When done correctly, the culture scan measures how well the college's policies and practices align with the core values of the institution.

Identify an equity coalition through governance and by mobilizing others. As leaders begin with the end in mind—an equity-centered institution—it's important to work with and through stakeholders to accomplish the goal (Covey, 2006). In the book, *The SPEED of Trust: The One Thing That Changes Everything,* Covey (2006) explained how trust—and the speed at which it is established with clients, employees, and all stakeholders—is the single most critical component of a successful leader and organization. Therefore, governance that embodies stakeholder engagement will be key to accomplishing the task. Governance in higher education may take many forms; however, it begins with the board and other constituent organizations (e.g., faculty senate) that may exist. When implementing a major change, leaders must take the time to examine the existing governance structures to include faculty, the board, and other internal groups. These structures can be used to mobilize others and create a guiding coalition to implement transformational change.

Form a strategic equity vision through governance with clear communication and intentional collaboration. Developing an equity-centered vision will take intentional collaboration and communication with all stakeholders. Engaging the guiding coalition to craft an equity vision ensures that all voices are part of the final product. The equity vision will be the way forward for the college. The equity vision serves as the college's bold statement to adhere to equitable processes, practices, and procedures in every way.

Communicate the equity vision through collaboration and the governance process. Moving an equity agenda forward will be met with resistance; therefore, a volunteer army that understands the vision will be critical to success. The name *volunteer army* suggests the exact intent. It is important to draft people who want to be involved in this work. Forcing a group to move the equity vision forward will not create the genuine passion necessary as people communicate the vision and collaborate with others. Using the volunteer army to clearly communicate and collaborate with other faculty and staff will create synergy around the topic.

Utilize institutional leadership and collaboration to empower employees for broad-based action. Leaders of the transformational change process must feel empowered to identify, investigate, and eradicate barriers that exist at the college. These barriers come in many forms (people, policies, practices, culture) that the guiding coalition will be able to identify and change. The barriers, as Maxwell (2007) in his *21 Irrefutable Laws of Leadership* refers to them, may be referenced as a *lid.* The lid is a constraint that is often a self-inflicted barrier. It can be as simple as the barrier of "we have always done it that way" that prevents change. Leaders who implement an equity agenda will have to examine all of those barriers, both apparent and transparent, and can strive toward removing them.

Generate short-term wins through relationship cultivation. As the equity agenda progresses, leaders of the effort must continue to build relationships throughout the institution and celebrate wins. The more internal and external stakeholders hear about the changes, some of which are low-hanging fruit, the more people will want to be connected to the work.

Sustain acceleration using institutional leadership. Once there is momentum at the institution around equity, leaders must model leadership behaviors that embed equity in their walk and talk. Transparency for the equity cause, advocacy for equity, and customer service that supports equity for all are some of the important leadership behaviors required to sustain acceleration. Leaders who do not continuously model equity will not be able to sustain their followers to support equity efforts at the college.

Institute change through governance and revamping the institutional infrastructure (as needed). Most institutions will likely make policy and procedural changes to support the equity agenda, especially in the student enrollment or employee recruitment process. At most community colleges, all policies have to be approved by the board, vetted through the internal constituent governance bodies, and approved at the executive level. Leaders should continue to utilize the governance process to implement the change to gain buy-in to any new policies and procedures.

While the equity-centered transformational change framework can be implemented as a step-by-step process, it does have the flexibility to be a situational change model. For example, as new barriers emerge, there may be a renewed need for urgency. If, say, a sense of urgency around student success data leads to understanding that the admission process is not fairly applied to all student groups, a new sense of urgency could develop to lead institutions toward a new "mini" change process within the overarching goal of developing an equity-centered institution. Here's the point: Community colleges are dynamic institutions, and the leadership of change and/or processes guiding the change process need to be equally dynamic.

By using the equity-centered transformational change framework, the nation's community colleges can remain focused on their original mission— open access to everyone! An equity-centered framework requires community colleges not only to support the removal of obstacles that students face getting into college but also ensure that support services are available to continue to empower students throughout the matriculation process. The equity model outlined in this text has the potential to transform institutions so that they are equipped to dismantle institutional inequities that prevent students from accomplishing their goals.

2

CREATE A SENSE OF URGENCY FOR EQUITY THROUGH THE EXISTING ORGANIZATIONAL CULTURE

Chapter highlights: In this chapter, we provide a guide for developing a sense of urgency to work toward becoming an equity-centered institution. To create a sense of urgency, the majority must buy in, which means examining the culture and assessing the readiness for change is very important!

Leadership focus areas: Organizational culture, student success, institutional leadership, institutional infrastructure, information, and analytics.

K otter's step of creating a sense of urgency discusses how leaders can "help others see the need for change through a bold, aspirational opportunity statement that communicates the importance of acting immediately" (Kotter, 1996, p. 44). In higher education, acting immediately just simply doesn't happen if the implementation is going to go well—the reality is that each institution must design specific action steps to create a sense of urgency.

There are several reasons we encourage institutions to launch their equity work with establishing a sense-of-urgency mind-set: (a) It sends a signal to stakeholders that the institution is focused; (b) it demonstrates the importance of the work and how it is linked to institution-wide initiatives and goals; and (c) it demonstrates that the institution has prioritized equity within the culture of the college. High-performing institutions, leaders, and teams flourish by operating under a sense-of-urgency mind-set. We encourage institutions to use our equity-centered transformational change framework (Figure 1.2) to move the equity work forward. Further, we use Kotter's sense-of-urgency approach for placing the "big idea" for change at the center of the institution's culture. To do so, CEOs and leadership teams must "embrace diversity as a focal point in the mission, vision, and values of the community college, and acknowledge the significance of the institution's past while charting a path forward for its future" (AACC, 2018, p. 5). In essence, the culture of the institution is vitally important to creating a sense of urgency. According to Kotter (2014), one of the mistakes in implementing change is neglecting to anchor changes firmly in the [institutional] culture. When equity guides the behavioral norms and "seeps into the very bloodstream" of the college, then the change will stick (Kotter, 2014, p. 14).

Organizations are filled with people who are complacent. Complacency in an institutional culture will create a stagnant state for the college (Kotter, 2014). There are many elements (internally and externally) that influence the culture of the organization. The extent to which leaders can embrace and implement transformational change depends primarily on their ability to understand the connectivity between cultural differences among employees such as communication, behaviors, beliefs, and values that are operating within the organization. Institutional culture is the driving force and focus for the sense of urgency. Creating a sense of urgency in the form of an equity plan will include identifying the equity challenge, assessing the institution's readiness for the transformation, and identifying champions to promote the change. We have identified three basic processes that institutions can use to create a sense of urgency for equity: (a) Identify the big equity challenges; (b) assess the institution's readiness for the equity transformation; and (c) identify champions.

Sense of Urgency, Step 1: Identify the "Big" Equity Challenges

Equity issues in higher education are complex, cutting across academic disciplines, sectors, and society as a whole. *Equity*, as defined in chapter 1, can be a complex challenge for many institutions. What is the equity challenge at your institution? This can be a hard question to answer as you scan the institution. Most institutions face similar challenges when launching equity initiatives. In theory, equity in community colleges would provide all learners everything they need to achieve academic success. But examining and defining institutional data alone is a challenge for some community colleges, and diagnosing the data and addressing the needs of individual students presents further challenges. When the data are examined, the achievement gaps for students of color are highly prevalent at too many colleges. The achievement gaps are, unfortunately, a common problem that can be addressed through the equity-centered transformational change model we outline in this text. We encourage institutions to examine achievement disparities as well as other equity issues at their institution before launching an equity agenda.

Equity challenges are visible throughout the institution in areas such as hiring practices, retention of employees, and delivery of services. With all these realities, how does one determine where to begin? As challenging as equity can be, the primary challenge for most institutions is developing an institutional culture centered on equity. Since moving equity to the center of the institution's culture is an evolutionary process, all of the other processes, interactions, and data should change over time; it will take time to infuse equity throughout the organization. Therefore, creating a sense of urgency is essentially about placing the equity efforts at the center of the institution's goals and strategic plan and using the data derived from the institution's review and from the analysis of the issues.

The big challenge for some community colleges in America is providing a quality student and employee experience (Bailey et al., 2015). A learner's experience determines whether the student returns next semester. Think about it: When you go into a grocery store, if the clerk is rude, you may not return to that store. The same can true in community colleges. Becoming an equity-centered institution can change perceptions and behaviors over time. By taking the time to assess the institution's readiness for the equity challenge, leadership teams will be able to confirm the basic equity challenges at the institution and develop results-oriented interventions.

Sense of Urgency, Step 2: Assess the Institution's Readiness for the Equity Transformation

In higher education, operating with a sense of urgency could mean the difference between a large number of students getting what they need to successfully navigate their student experience and missing out on opportunities to accomplish their goals. It can mean knowing when to offer a service and focus making that service available. It can also mean knowing there will be times when the institution may have to discontinue services that are not working, redesign programs and services (Bailey et al., 2015), and get what needs to be done first *done*. But, how can leaders know whether the institution is ready to take on a transformational change effort?

The leadership required to assess the institution's equity challenges can be a humbling experience for both new and veteran leaders. When a new CEO enters the position, the experience may be humbling because the leader may be expected to lead the institution into a new era that is remarkably different from the past and in which the leader may experience difficulty navigating the new waters. In other words, new leaders may experience some "bruises" along the way. For a veteran CEO, some of the items uncovered in an equity readiness analysis may reveal problems that were not under the current administration's control, so ushering the college into the future may require admitting that previous administrators may have made mistakes in their efforts to lead the change process (AACC, 2018). The institutional leader's tenure should not be a factor in determining the institution's readiness for launching the equity assessment. Whether leadership is new or senior, the goal is to strive for a comprehensive equity-centered institution; therefore, the assessment must always be comprehensive.

It's important to recognize that a quantitative and qualitative assessment approach is recommended in order to collect the necessary institutional data that reveals a sense of urgency for change. The following are initial questions that may be considered to develop an equity-centered inquiry:

1. What is the institution's capacity for data collection?
2. Do the faculty, staff, and administration (by employee group) model the student population?
3. What are the success, retention, and completion rates for students when disaggregated by age, race, and socioeconomic class?
4. What is the turnover rate of employees by employee group type?

Many institutions get stuck on the first question, feeling that the college does not have "good" data. The last three questions are "initial" questions that institutions must address when launching the equity work. These questions are necessary as they help the institution capture essential baseline information about the readiness of the institution to take on the equity work. Once the data collected from the analysis of these questions has been reviewed, more questions will likely emerge to help shape the narrative around a comprehensive equity agenda.

One of the authors once worked at an Achieving the Dream institution where she learned that leaders cannot allow the data they don't have to keep them from moving toward what they wanted to learn. We encourage institutions to use the data they have to press forward—don't waste valuable time looking for data that you don't have. It is what it is. Part of the transformational change may be addressing the institutional data collection and reporting capacity: the data warehouse, integration of platforms, and technological interface. The point is not to allow the current state of the

Institutional Research Office to stifle future progress. According to Ewell (2010), community colleges are just beginning to position themselves to be in this space. Ewell (2010) suggested that some of the data collected by colleges is never used and that their reasons for not using the data may be as simple as lack of knowledge and awareness about how to link data to presenting problems and to shortfalls in campus analytical and institutional research capacity.

In this age of declining resources—when so many institutions are asked to respond to competing challenges for resources—we acknowledge that many institutions do not have access or the time to identify tools to conduct institutional readiness assessments. We have developed a tool to help institutions move quickly through the institutional readiness process. For the qualitative component of the data collection, we have adapted NERCHE's self-assessment rubric to an institutional assessment rubric for institutionalizing a comprehensive equity agenda in community colleges (hereafter referred to as Institutional Self-Assessment for Equity; see Appendix A).

The institutional equity assessment is a tool that leaders can use to examine the landscape and culture of the college by gathering perceptions of internal stakeholders. It consists of four major elements: dimensions, components, stages of readiness, and evidence indicators. The rubric contains six dimensions and several components related to equity constructs for each dimension. For each component, a four-stage continuum of development was developed. The progression from stage one to stage four indicates the institution's readiness toward fully institutionalizing equity (NERCHE, 2019).

Our Approach for Using the Institutional Equity Assessment

The primary purposes of using the institutional equity assessment are to determine the institution's readiness to take a transformational equity challenge and to be a tool to facilitate the college's ability to change and assess existing processes and resources available to support equity efforts. Using the rubric may prove useful in identifying gaps in the institution's structure, processes, and culture that require radical transformation to ensure that equity is at the center of the decision-making process. We make two recommendations for taking the assessment:

1. In multi-campus/college systems, conduct a district-wide assessment. If the institution is going to make transformational change, it cannot occur on an island.
2. Create broad engagement and include as many stakeholders as possible.

The institutional equity assessment is a tool that should be approached like a research project; in fact, it is a research project focused on learning whether the institution is ready for transformational change through an equity lens. As such, all research projects have a protocol. A *protocol* is the manner in which the research is administered. In this case, there are three approaches suggested by NERCHE (2019):

1. Administrative review: The senior-level leadership conducts the assessment using their worldview to respond to the rubric from their perspective as well as their perception of the unit supervised (e.g., Academic Affairs).
2. Broad-based engagement: Individuals from many levels of the institution are engaged in responding to the rubric.
3. Limited broad-based engagement: Individuals from many levels of the institution are engaged but on a limited scale, meaning that there may be a limited number of participants per employee group (e.g., staff, faculty, administrators, students) who complete the rubric.

We strongly recommend the college consider the culture of the college when determining the best protocol to use.

Description of Institutional Equity Assessment Elements

There are many assessment tools on the market; however, one that is simple and practical is the model adapted from NERCHE, the "Self-Assessment Rubric for the Institutionalization of Diversity, Equity, and Inclusion in Higher Education." Through four dimensions—faculty support, staff support, student support, and administrative leadership—an institution can determine its progress on components of the dimensions through a framework of whether the behaviors are emerging, developing, or transforming. Through these processes, it is extremely important not to confuse *diversity*, *inclusion*, and *equity*; these terms mean three different things but are interrelated.

The institutional equity assessment consists of a framework that includes four primary elements: six dimensions, components for each dimension, stage of development, and indicators. It is important to note that any college using this rubric should modify it to reflect its culture; however, we strongly encourage that the framework remains the same. For example, there may be instances where the components suggested in the sample (see Table 2.1) omit one or more ideas that are key to the colleges' institutionalization efforts (NERCHE, 2019). Likewise, colleges may

TABLE 2.1

Guide for Institutional Self-Assessment for Equity

			Dimension I: Philosophy of Equity		
Components	Stage 1: Emerging	Stage 2: Developing	Stage 3: Transforming	Stage 4: Informing	Indicators
Definition of equity	There is no college-wide definition of equity.	Conversations regarding a definition of equity have occurred.	There is a college-wide formal definition of equity. The philosophy of equity is being incorporated into policies and procedures at the institution.	The formal definition has been integrated into all policies and procedures. The formal definition has been communicated broadly through various mediums.	
Inclusion of equity in the strategic plan	The college does not have equity included in the strategic plan.	There are goals centered on equity being developed at the institution.	The strategic plan has been revised to include equity-centered goals.	The revised strategic plan has been broadly shared throughout the institution.	
Alignment of equity with the institutional mission and values	The college does not have institutional values centered on equity.	There are conversations regarding the development of college-wide values that include equity.	Formal college-wide values have been created.	The college values are integrated into practices and behaviors at the institution.	

choose to add components for the same reason, but the dimensions and the stages should remain the same.

Dimensions, as applied in the assessment, refer to a group of connected ideas in one space, a dimension. The following is a description of each dimension included in the institutional equity assessment:

- Dimension 1: Philosophy of equity. The first aspect of a transformational change process focused on equity is ensuring that the institution has a common understanding and definition of equity. The components assessed in this dimension should be high-level ideas that will guide the college toward a common understanding of equity (e.g., strategic planning, mission, and accreditation).
- Dimension 2: Faculty support for and involvement in equity. In most colleges, the faculty is the core voice (either supportive or resisting change). If there is going to be a true transformation at the institution, the faculty must be engaged. Components in this dimension evaluate the level of knowledge and engagement of faculty regarding equity—their ownership of equity at the institution (NERCHE, 2019).
- Dimension 3: Teaching, research, and service supporting equity. There are many items that can be perceived as "initiatives." To avoid this type of thinking in the equity process, the items in this area should point to the integration of equity into key, intimate areas of the institution that focus on students. In this dimension, we are also looking to measure the level of engagement by faculty in the implementation and advancement of pedagogy, research, and scholarship (NERCHE, 2019).
- Dimension 4: Staff engagement and involvement in equity is similar to dimension 3 but different in that the focus of the dimension is on staff and their level of engagement in the implementation of equity.
- Dimension 5: For all community colleges, students are at the core of the mission. Therefore, colleges should examine the degree to which students are provided the opportunity or are engaged in learning about equity through cocurricular experiences (NERCHE, 2019).
- Dimension 6: Administrative leadership and institutional support for equity. Transformation of this magnitude takes considerable resources, support, and accountability. The administrative leadership must be committed to equity for success (NERCHE, 2019).

All of these dimensions are critical to the overall transformation. Some may have more weight than others given the institutional culture. Considering the culture in this process should guide the weight of each dimension.

The second element of the institutional equity assessment is the components. The components are the elements rated through each stage. The components should cascade from the dimensions. Each set of components characterizes a dimension (NERCHE, 2019). The components are an aspect of the institutional equity assessment that may shift as they are driven by institutional culture. The components may also change based on the major goal for equity. If the college is solely focused on improving equity with students, then the components will strictly address those aspects that lead to an improved student experience. However, if an institution is focused on equity in the student and employee experience, then the components would encompass those elements as well. In the end, the internal stakeholders may likely add to the suggestions that follow or modify language given the culture at the college:

- Dimension 1: Philosophy of equity. The recommended components are a common definition of equity; a strategic plan that includes equity; aligning equity with the institutional mission; aligning equity with education reform efforts practiced at the college, aspects of accreditation, and areas where equity can be included; and historical and geographical contexts for better understanding equity (NERCHE, 2019).
- Dimension 2: Faculty support for equity. The recommended components are faculty knowledge and awareness of equity, faculty involvement and support of equity, faculty leadership around equity matters, faculty rewards/recognition for work in equity, and faculty development incentives in equity (NERCHE, 2019).
- Dimension 3: Curriculum, pedagogy, and research regarding equity. The recommended components are knowledge and awareness of equity in relation to individual disciplines, faculty teaching and learning strategies that include equity, and student learning outcomes that focus on equity such as closing achievement gaps (NERCHE, 2019).
- Dimension 4: Staff engagement and involvement in equity: The recommended components are staff knowledge and awareness of equity, staff engagement and involvement in equity-focused activities, and staff rewards for work that fosters an equity-centered culture (NERCHE, 2019).
- Dimension 5: Student support for and involvement in equity through cocurricular activities. The recommended components are student knowledge and awareness of equity-focused events and activities, involvement and engagement in equity-focused activities, student

leadership opportunities focused on equity, and student rewards for research or leadership in equity (NERCHE, 2019).

- Dimension 6: Administrative leadership and institutional support for equity. The recommended components are coordination of institutional efforts focused on equity, policy-making entities, hiring practices focused on equity, hiring and retention plans focused on equity, and funding to support equity initiatives (NERCHE, 2019).

Once the components are identified and confirmed, each component should be tested through each stage of the equity rubric (see Table 2.1).

The third element of the institutional equity assessment is the stages of institutional readiness. By measuring where the institution stands with every component, the college can establish a sense of urgency for implementing equity. Each leadership team must have the adaptability and competencies to lead the institution through a transformational change process. The leadership at each institution must understand the institution's readiness for that change is critical to the success of the overall process. The equity rubric includes four stages by which each dimension is measured:

1. Stage 1: Emerging. At this stage, the college may be beginning to recognize equity as a strategic priority.
2. Stage 2: Developing. At this stage, the college is in the process of developing a process for becoming an equity-centered institution.
3. Stage 3: Transforming. At this stage, the college is in the process of implementing the process for becoming an equity-centered institution.
4. Stage 4: Informing. At this stage, the college is institutionalizing an equity-centered agenda.

The last element of the rubric is the indicators, which refers to the evidence that supports the perspective provided relative to the stage in which the college is currently operating. Indicators should be in the form of tangible evidence such as equity programming, a specific professional development opportunity, or other factors that contribute to the equity agenda. Tangible types of evidence serve as good indicators of where equity gaps may exist. The dimensions, components, stages, and indicators combine to create a comprehensive equity assessment that will provide essential data to move forward with a focused equity agenda (see Table 2.1).

After the institution has assessed its readiness for implementing an equity-centered agenda, the data should be triangulated to identify big themes and/or gaps for moving forward with launching the equity initiative. Other existing forms of data can also be used. For example, the results of an existing survey of entering student engagement (SENSE) or community college survey of student engagement (CCSSE) or employee satisfaction survey can be used to inform equity gaps.

When one institution in Texas used the institutional equity assessment survey to assess its equity readiness, they learned that professional development was a common theme across all assessments (employee satisfaction and the institutional equity assessment). In this case, the institution's sense of urgency and key component of the equity agenda focused on professional development. What did the college in Texas accomplish? They tapped into the "voice" of the college and were able to get buy-in around equity-centered professional development.

With data from these assessments, leaders will be armed with information that can create a sense of urgency across a broad group of issues. The institution will have concrete data to share with stakeholders who are engaged in developing a plan from the beginning. The next tough decision after the assessment is to determine who will lead the effort. It takes a special individual or group of individuals to champion this work!

In chapter 10, "Promote Equity in the Field," we profile the work of one national association, three community colleges, and the survey results from three different institutional types to get input from practitioners in the field. Our intent was to collect data from the field to get a pulse of current equity efforts and practices from different institutional perspectives. The discussion in the college profiles focuses on how the colleges launched their equity efforts. All the questions on the institutional equity assessment survey focused on the equity work taking place at the institution and were tied to the specific objectives of learning from the practitioners in the field.

Sense of Urgency, Step 3: Identify a Champion

At most institutions, most of the assessment practices (data collection and analysis) will likely be conducted by personnel in the Institutional Research Office. After the institution has committed to launching an equity agenda, it will need a courageous leader—a champion to promote the work. A champion is someone who is passionate about equity, understands the institutional culture, and has credibility with all internal stakeholders. A champion is also someone who is a decision-maker at the college, someone who can identify and acquire resources necessary for moving the effort forward. If the CEO can find all these characteristics in one individual, congratulations. More than likely, there will be at least two, no more than three, champions identified. The president must support the role of the champions so that constituent groups at the institution understand that the champion(s) have the authority to conduct the equity work. Again, working through existing institutional governance structure is a logical first step when launching the equity work at the institution. Typically, there is a governance structure at the college; it is wise to begin leading the change process toward equity centeredness by tapping into that existing governance structure for leadership talent. For example, consider the following:

- Senior leader: This champion should have access to resources and be empowered to make decisions. This senior leader will also keep the CEO and the rest of the senior leadership team informed about the progress equity initiatives. Most importantly, the senior leader should be an influencer, a person within this small group who can influence stakeholders to move forward with the equity agenda.
- Faculty member: This champion should be a good listener and highly revered (trusted) by the faculty. It is important for the faculty member to be an influencer but in a different way from the administrator. In the case of faculty, influence should be the ability to influence colleagues to become involved in the equity work at the college. In most community colleges, getting faculty groups to embrace transformational change is usually the most difficult challenge for the institution (Rowley et al., 1997). This reluctance to change may be due to a wide range of factors. In some cases, the majority of faculty members are simply focused on teaching rather than making the connection of how changes in pedagogy and curriculum can impact the learning experience for students. A faculty champion who is passionate about this work will be able to collaborate with other faculty to see the importance of making changes to enhance the total teaching and learning environment at the institution.
- Midlevel manager: This champion should possess the same listening and trustworthy attributes as the senior leaders and faculty; however, this individual will provide the frontline contact with faculty and other support personnel who implement and manage the change at the operational level. The midlevel manager's proximity to the operational activities makes them a valuable asset to the implementation team.

After the champions have been identified, this core group will continue to explain the sense of urgency for launching the equity agenda to the college-wide community. The first step is for the champions to synthesize the data into a digestible, meaningful fashion for planning. Most college employees are not unaccustomed to seeing and using data to inform decision-making.

The team of champions must strive to promote the use of data at the institution. We encourage teams to start the equity work by asking a few basic data-use questions: What does the data mean for faculty, staff, midlevel leadership, and students? How does the data impact their daily work and the student experience? How do we know? The answers to these simple questions will inform a design that has meaning for stakeholders and the institution. The data must be presented in a fashion that raises the level of urgency (Kotter, 2014).

Kotter (1996) asks, how much urgency is enough? You will know there has been enough urgency when complacency has been removed. According to Kotter, when you have the majority of stakeholders (75%) sold that the status quo is no longer acceptable, you have reached a point where you can move to the next phase in the transformation process.

3

IDENTIFY AN EQUITY COALITION THROUGH GOVERNANCE AND BY MOBILIZING OTHERS

Chapter highlights: In this chapter, we discuss the need for competent leadership to develop a guiding coalition that will make transformational change happen. By finding the right people, creating trust, and developing a common goal, a strong force can be created to move the equity agenda forward.

Leadership focus areas: Governance, institutional policy, legislation, institutional leadership, advocacy, mobilizing others, and communication.

In chapter 2 we explained how the first step in becoming an equity-centered institution required senior leaders to create a sense of urgency to gain stakeholders' attention about the need for becoming equity centered. Once the sense of urgency has been established, steps must be taken to build a guiding coalition. It is based on the principle of engagement at all levels of the institution. Using Kotter's (2014) "guiding coalition" concept, moving forward, we refer to this coalition as the *equity oversight team* (EOT).

While there are different levels of engagement that will occur throughout the transformation process in becoming an equity-centered institution, the first level of engagement focuses on creating the EOT. In the process of leading change, some will have a greater impact on the outcome than others. We encourage institutions to create an EOT to help facilitate reaching the desired goal.

Identifying the EOT through broad-based engagement is necessary for gathering ideas that will have a broad-based impact on the institution. The EOT will literally guide the work toward becoming an equity-centered institution, further deepening the engagement as institutions move through the transformation process.

Developing the EOT is where the synergy of the AACC leadership competencies and Kotter's (2014) leading change model can be aligned. The alignment of the competencies and associated behaviors demonstrates the leadership competencies needed to develop the EOT. Based on our experience in the field and our research, we propose a model, "Leadership Competencies for Developing an Equity Oversight Team for Becoming an Equity-Centered Institution." Table 3.1 reflects the ideal characteristics of an EOT and their alignment with the AACC leadership competencies that have been adapted to the leadership behaviors needed for equity-centered effort. As the champions move through these steps to identify the guiding coalition represented in column one, the leadership competencies illustrated in columns two and three represent the skills the champion should be looking for as they build the EOT.

Since the EOT is the primary body that will be engaging the college community in becoming an equity-centered institution, the senior leaders should consider these leadership competencies as they move through

TABLE 3.1
Leadership Capacity for Developing an EOT

Steps for developing an equity oversight team	Competency area	Focused competency (FC)/leadership behavior (LB)
Find the right people	Governance	FC: Organizational structure of the community college LB: Review the institution's organizational structure to identify the right people with influence
		FC: Governance structure LB: Continue to embrace your institution's governance structure to ensure representation is included in the guiding coalition
Create trust	Institutional leadership	FC: Be an influencer LB: Assert your influence to advance the equity agenda
		FC: Lead by example LB: Exhibit integrity and ethics in decision-making as you guide the process

the transformation process. The following section describes each step in developing a guiding coalition through broad-based engagement prepared to move the institution toward becoming an equity-centered institution (see Table 3.1).

Find the Right People

As the senior leaders develop an EOT, it is important that they find the right people to advocate, lead, and, in some cases, implement the equity transformation processes. Becoming an equity-centered institution requires people who have position power, equity expertise, credibility, and leadership (Kotter, 2014). Institutions are encouraged to look at all levels of the institution for representation on the EOT. It is important to strive for a perfect balance of representation on an EOT. A perfect balance may not be defined by the number of people, but rather by the tasks that need to be accomplished. In other words, the perfect balance is contingent on the needs of the institution where equity is concerned.

To determine the perfect balance, ask yourself, "Where is the largest equity impact needed?" The response to this question is an iterative process to an extent, for as the process evolves, a gap may be identified where new people are needed to get the work done. It's important to do the best analysis about the greatest impact early in the process because the answer will inform the representation on the team in terms of position power, experience, and credibility. For example, one president may recommend a perfect balance to be the number of participants from different stakeholder groups because both the student and employee experience are equally in need of change. At other institutions, the student experience may be the focus, so the perfect balance would rely more on those who have direct experience with students.

Once the senior leaders have determined the right balance for the EOT, institutions are encouraged to use the institution's organizational and governance structures to identify the right composition for the team. Depending on the institutional culture, the process for identifying participants may vary. Institutional leaders are strongly encouraged to evaluate the organizational structures to identify potential candidates for the team. Leaders are encouraged to invite the governance leadership to the table to collaboratively confirm and further discuss representation on the team. At most institutions, the governance leaders can be the strongest advocates for change in the institution; incorporate them into the change process and more buy-in from stakeholders will likely follow.

Create Trust

While trust may need attention in some institutions, it is necessary to motivate a team and move the EOT forward (Kotter, 2014). Trust is the primary element that will lead to a productive team. Trust is especially important when striving to become an equity-centered institution. In order for stakeholders to embrace an equity agenda, they must understand and trust the institution's data (Johnson, 2014). Institutions are encouraged to start building trust by using the institution's data as a focal point for the conversations around equity-centered outcomes. By building trust around the institution's data, senior leaders, champions, and the EOT will be empowered and can work together to build trust throughout the institution. Leaders must demonstrate word and action alignment in their everyday activities—stakeholders are watching. If employees do not trust the leadership team, they are not likely to get engaged with the equity agenda. The authors have observed that in cases where institutions lack engaged employees, the institution has a trust problem rather than an engagement problem. Be mindful that trust is not something that can be bought or sold to employees. The best way to engage employees in equity-centered work is for senior leaders to foster a trustworthy environment.

To create trust, senior leaders must demonstrate trustworthy leadership practices. First, everyone involved in leadership roles for advancing the institution toward becoming an equity-centered institution must be an influencer. Maxwell (2004) says, "If you don't have influence, you will never be able to lead others" (p. 23). For example, the members of the EOT must embody some type of influence; it may be the ability to influence others into action or it may be the ability to acquire the resources to support the equity agenda, but influence is required. Not only is it required, but the coalition will have to learn to skillfully use its influence as a unit and as individual members. It is important for team members to represent the goals of the equity team rather than their personal egos. People can sense ego and will not receive it well.

Second, all members of the EOT must lead by example. If the members of the team are sharing the ideals of equity, they must model the behavior that is aligned with equity principles. Sometimes the behavior may be a coordinated effort by the team, or it may be demonstrated at an individual member level. For example, if a person on the EOT is serving on a hiring committee where equitable practices are not being applied in the search process and preventing a diverse pool to emerge, they have a responsibility to model the way by bringing it to the search committee's attention. It is not uncommon to see the inequity and the unintentional impact of some practices at institutions; however, once the institution is educated on the common definition of equity, it's important that all stakeholders practice courageous conversations around equity and incorporate equitable practices into the day-to-day work of institutions.

Third, the EOT must develop and utilize problem-solving and conflict management techniques. Given the complexity and lack of understanding regarding equity, conflict is likely to emerge. Leaders of transformational change for equity have to be bold and, as appropriate, identify alternative paths and solutions. Let's return to the hiring committee example. Often staff members serving on selection committees will not speak up because of their perception of lack of authority due to their position. They may not feel empowered to identify unequitable practices. However, part of the EOT's role requires them to train stakeholders on how to embrace equity practices to learn how to boldly implement the practices in a respectful way. In a situation where a staff member serving on a hiring committee exposes unequitable practices, they should point to the evidence of the unfair practice upon discovering the inequity. Always allow the evidence to speak; it's the best way to resolve conflict.

Fourth, and probably most importantly, the EOT must practice transparency. Especially in a culture where trust is not prevalent, it is extremely important to be transparent. What does this really mean? It means that the coalition will have to lead by sharing everything—the good, the bad, and the ugly. When an institution enters an equity-focused journey, often what emerges from the qualitative and quantitative data is ugly (low student outcomes such as retention and graduation rates). Some of these conversations about data show the disparities in student outcomes among students of color and other learners. While many institutions are not prepared to discuss race-related problems, it's important to be transparent and share the data so that everyone is informed about the scope of the issues the institution is facing. Most institutional researchers are trained to share data with constituent groups even when some of the data may not be what stakeholders believe to be true about their institution. It is important for senior leaders to support an environment where the instruction research team can present data in a way that informs the college's story and connects the data to the equity issues, vision, and mission of the institution.

Senior leaders and the EOT members are encouraged to be transparent about where the institution is in the equity journey and what it will take to transform the institution. The key leadership competencies that come into play at this stage are communication, institutional leadership, advocacy, and mobilizing others. Stakeholders must be given the information to understand what is at stake and what it will take to transform the institution. In addition, the EOT members will need to be transparent about the process of becoming an equity-centered institution. The EOT members must work as a cohesive team to clearly communicate all aspects of the change model moving forward. People will appreciate the raw honesty, which will likely lead to more buy-in.

Foster Team Building

The senior leadership team cannot lead the college toward becoming an equity-centered institution alone. The success of a transformational change effort such as becoming an equity-centered institution largely depends on the engagement and the attention senior leaders give to team-building efforts. The importance of team building is sometimes minimized, and this omission frequently leads to failed transformational efforts. To foster team building for a group striving toward an equity-centered institution, mobilizing others and institutional leadership are the competencies required.

Kotter (2014) suggests that the best team building occurs during off-site retreats over 3 to 6 days with about 50 people. The value of being together and being focused on equity issues in the institution has a lot of value. In these types of retreats, not only is the team focused on the equity topic, but it is also an opportunity to truly develop and strengthen the team for the work to come. Kotter's suggestion of a retreat is a good one, but this is another instance where institutional culture is very important. In some cultures, spending the money for an off-site retreat and taking employees away for 5 straight days is not acceptable. In today's cost-conscious environments, we know there are institutional cultures that will not support an off-site leadership retreat. So, how do we get to team training considering the institutional culture?

The value of the champions in promoting the equity agenda process becomes even more evident when it requires institution-wide support of an event, policy, or practice. In this discussion, we continue to draw on AACC's leadership competencies. In order to move toward an equity-centered institution, there must be evidence of AACC's institutional leadership and advocacy competency. Specifically, the champions must support team building and advocate for the team-building forum. Champions should consider strategies to accomplish the goal by supporting the equity agenda and team through the culture. In doing so, leadership training may take on a variety of formats contingent on the culture of the institution. Some institutions have solved fiscal concerns about off-site retreats by holding their retreats at an off-site space donated by external partners. Others have solved concerns about time away from the institutions by holding the team training over a period of months (once per week over a period of 5 weeks) rather than 5 consecutive days.

With this alternative model, there is still enough compression of time and focus on the topic as to not lose the synergy needed to move the work forward. However, selecting an off-site location is very important (that element should not be lost) because it provides the space that team members need to focus on the issues and prevents them from running to their offices while the retreat is still in session.

The team-building retreat presents an opportunity for the senior leaders and champions to enhance the leadership skill that AACC (2018) identifies as *stakeholder mobilization*. Senior leaders and champions must take this opportunity to welcome all stakeholders to the table and be willing to be vulnerable in expressing the need for support for the equity agenda. In essence, this is a professional development opportunity for the attendees; it is also an opportunity for the champions to model the advocacy behavior that the team will need to demonstrate once they are deployed throughout the institution as equity advocates.

It's important to note that team building is not a one-time event; it should continue over time. The team-building retreat is the "kick-off" event. The result of continuing to foster team building is strengthened communication, a mutual understanding of equity, and improved trust. These three elements will be critical to developing the team. The champions must exhibit the leadership to lead to these outcomes. To accomplish these outcomes, senior leaders and the champions can gain momentum around a discussion of the common goals for the equity work at the institution.

Develop a Common Goal

We have observed that among all institutional types there can be a gap between aspirations of the leaders and the employees. We encourage leaders to bring all stakeholders together in pursuit of the common goal of becoming an equity-centered institution. (See Figure 3.1.) As trust continues to be developed and the EOT is established, it is now time to mobilize the group around the development of a common goal. Institutions can move toward becoming an equity-centered institution by defining equity and setting common goals. Institutions are encouraged to use the information in this book and the results of the institutional equity assessment to develop a process to attain their equity goals. The senior leaders and champions must model passionate advocacy for equity and guide the oversight team toward a common

Figure 3.1. Equity-centered goal setting process.

equity-centered goal. The goal is important because it "binds individuals together on guiding change" (Kotter, 2014, p. 67).

While we know the goal—to become an equity-centered institution— what does that really mean, and how does this coalition communicate the goal to the broader community? The ability of the senior leadership team to demonstrate the leadership competencies of communications, advocacy, and mobilizing others will be central to reaching the goal of becoming an equity-centered institution (AACC, 2018).

College-wide conversation about the big impact regarding equity needs to occur. The following is a suggested strategy for implementing a conversation for reaching a common goal. We recommend that EOT conduct a common goal-setting session that utilizes institutional data to identify equity gaps at the institution. This might take the form of a special workshop or seminar.

We propose four strategies for institutions to reach a common goal.

Strategy 1: Review the Data

The qualitative and quantitative data the institution collects must be presented in a display that can be easily digested. It is recommended that all data are presented: the institutional equity assessment, the student institutional data, the employee institutional data, Community College Survey of Student Engagement (CCSSE), Survey of Entering Student Engagement (SENSE), and other data inputs available. Team members must review and analyze the data as a collective group.

After the data have been analyzed, we recommend creating data teams and assign each group one data set, such as employee demographics, graduation, or workforce data. Depending on the size and scope of the institution, data teams may look different. The purpose of a data team is to guide future conversations and champion the cause that may emerge from the data. Data team members can be a very valuable resource as the broad engagement continues.

Once the data teams have been created, groups must be provided time to digest, synthesize, and translate the data into meaning. Simple guiding questions may be given to each group to guide an exercise where participants focus on the following questions:

- What do the data illustrate on the surface?
- What impact do these data have on the college?
- What impact do these data have in my daily work?
- What impact do these data have on the student and employee experience?

The answers to these questions will stimulate a great discussion in the next step, which is the goal-setting process.

Strategy 2: Synthesize the Outputs From the Data

After about an hour of the data teams working individually (provide more time if necessary), the champions have to utilize the leadership competency of communication by inviting each group to share the outputs from the discussion that took place in strategy 1. Active listening from all team members will be key during this stage. A natural human reaction is to respond to what is presented; true leaders listen and guide the conversation and allow others to chime in, creating a rich discussion. The team member's role in this forum is to guide, ask questions, and stay on task. Once all outputs are presented, the team leaders should work *with* the group to identify common themes from the impact questions. It is important to allow the themes to emerge from the group as guided by the session leaders.

Strategy 3: Identify the Area of Big Impact

After synthesizing the data, themes should emerge from the analysis. Institutional leaders will need to demonstrate confidence in what they see to move the EOT forward. Confidence is simple: State the position and follow with the question, "What do you think?" In taking this approach, try to drill down to three themes in the data; these themes should be the areas of big impact. The challenge in this part of the discussion is elevating the discussion into big ideas that everyone agrees on.

This step where the big idea has been identified is also a good stopping point if the retreat is being broken into segments or if you are simply conducting the session as a standalone workshop. Stopping here will also allow attendees time to digest what has been discussed thus far. Finally, a homework assignment, maybe through an online forum, can be given to the team around developing a formal, college-wide definition. In essence, where do these three big ideas point the focus of the institution where equity is concerned? The answer takes careful deliberation in order to more clearly focus the equity conversation at the college.

Strategy 4: Generate Consensus on the Formal College-Wide Definition of Equity

At this point the coalition should have given some thought to a college-wide, formal definition that is lifted from the principle of equity (fairness, access to the same opportunities). Those three themes, combined with the equity principle, should, at a very high level, lead to a definition of equity (e.g., "At Dream College USA, equity refers to parity in all processes, procedures, and practices that impact the student and employee experience and eliminate unintentional disparities"). As team members facilitating this discussion, a draft definition must have consensus among the group before moving to the goal.

Strategy 5: Develop a Common Goal for the EOT

The goal in this sense is the idea that binds the team together (Kotter, 2014). After reviewing the data, synthesizing the data, and identifying major themes that lead to a college-wide definition, what is the EOT's goal? Based on Kotter's (2014) leading change work, we believe that it is the extent to which the institution can demonstrate a commitment to excellence in the implementation of the equity agenda The point here is for the EOT to generate excitement around an approach to this work that will keep them moving forward.

Engaging the college in an equity agenda by creating and developing an EOT is a heavy lift; however, with the right people and the leadership team demonstrating the leadership competencies, the load can become a little lighter. While some of these factors were predeveloped, not predetermined, it is important to build the team's buy-in on the definition, be transparent about the data, have courageous conversations regarding the data, and lead the coalition toward the area of big impact. Once the area of greatest impact is determined, the goal can be articulated to the wider college community.

Some institutions may choose to hire a consultant to guide the big impact discussion. However, if the champions have been selected correctly and they bring influence and experience to the conversation, their credibility and trust is priceless. Let's put this formula into practice.

4

FORM A STRATEGIC EQUITY VISION THROUGH GOVERNANCE WITH CLEAR COMMUNICATION AND INTENTIONAL COLLABORATION

Chapter highlights: In this chapter, we discuss processes institutions can undergo to develop and link their vision statements to equity. We also provide a set of guiding questions for institutions to use as they determine ways to engage stakeholders in the work of creating an equity statement aligned with the core values of the institution.

Leadership focus areas: Governance, institutional policy, and legislation; institutional leadership; advocacy, mobilizing others; fundraising and relationship cultivation; communications; and collaboration.

Vision is an important aspect of the process of becoming an equity-centered institution. Typically, the institution's vision statement describes the aspirational goals for the institutions. When forming equity vision statements, we encourage institutions to project what they hope to achieve when they successfully fulfil their equity goals. The equity vision statement may describe the institution's core values, its long-term objectives, or the impact on students by becoming an equity-centered institution. Achieving the Dream (n.d.a) leads the largest network of community colleges in the United States. Since its founding, Achieving the Dream (ATD) has been a strong and vocal advocate for access and equity. In chapter 10, "Promote Equity in the Field," Karen Stout, president and CEO of Achieving the Dream, describes ATD's intensive efforts to create a statement that clearly communicates ATD's fundamental commitment to equity.

As exemplified in the ATD equity statement, people need to *see* something that will inspire them to follow the leader. Kotter (2014) posits that "clarifying the direction of change [by articulating a vision] is important because, more often than not, people disagree on direction, or are confused, or wonder whether significant change is really necessary" (p. 71). Based on our experiences, equity is a topic that will likely be met with resistance from different stakeholders. Establishing a clear vision collaboratively will reduce the resistance. The engagement of stakeholders will give them the opportunity to determine the role they may play in advancing the equity agenda. After the EOT has identified a common equity goal for the institution, the institution can take the next big step in becoming an equity-centered institution. Using the leadership competencies of communication, advocacy, and mobilizing/motivating others, institutional leadership, collaboration, and governance will undergird the guiding coalition's approach in developing an equity vision.

Linking the Vision to Equity

Kotter (2014) defines *vision* as a picture of the future that comments on why people should be motivated to create that future. The key strategy for creating a vision is to motivate people into action. A vision also communicates in a very bold way the ideals that are important for the college to advance. Here's the connection: A lot of work has been done to establish that the institution has either procedural, policy-driven, or behavior-driven gaps in equity. Why wouldn't the institution create a vision focused on equity?

The other aspect that the EOT needs to consider is in what direction the vision should be developed. In other words, is this an initiative-specific vision that flows from the college's strategic plan, or is this a big enough issue that it is the vision for the college? Given that the development of the vision for the college is typically led by the CEO and supported by the board of trustees, the vision question may be best led by the CEO. However, for the purpose of this discussion, we will work under the assumption that the equity-focused vision will align with the vision of the college, with the understanding that it not the sole vision for the college. This approach should be used when "facilitating major changes by motivating action that is not necessarily in people's short-term self-interests" (Kotter, 2014, p. 72). Developing feasible, focused, and flexible equity vision is the best path with the least resistance.

The EOT will have to lead the college down this path toward becoming an equity-centered institution.

Creating an Equity-Centered Vision

A good approach to starting the visioning process is to work on the equity vision during a team development training session or team retreat. In the leadership training example that we provided, the visioning session can be day 3 of the offsite team meetings. The same leadership competencies required to develop the common goal will be needed to develop the equity-focused vision. Creating the vision is the point where the process starts to feel real for many people. Therefore, the communication competencies of the senior leaders and equity team members are very important during this stage.

The team members leading this discussion should always speak with confidence, communicate clearly, and listen carefully. It's important to remember that the EOT champions and senior leaders will be communicating this vision as well, so continuing to demonstrate a spirit of advocacy that mobilizes people around the equity issues. According to AACC (2018), advocacy is an essential leadership skill. As such, effective community college leader understands, commits to, and advocates for the mission, vision, and goals of the community college on the local, state, and national level. At times, it may present a challenge for all team members to keep the focus on the common goal because they may face situations where others may ask questions about individual behavior rather than the change process (Kotter, 2014).

During the visioning session, participants can be reminded of the work done so far, showing the trail that led to the three big themes developed at the common goal identification session. Since it is important to keep everyone engaged on this issue, session leaders may consider asking, "Did we cover everything? Is there something anyone thinks we should add now that you have time to talk about it?" The facilitators must possess the communication and leadership competencies to keep the participants focused on creating the equity vision.

The power of the EOT and the balanced voices it represents become extremely valuable as the visioning exercise continues. Those diverse voices will confirm whether there is a common equity-focused vision that is imaginable, feasible, and communicative (Kotter, 2014). The EOT should consider the following as ground rules to developing an equity-focused vision:

- Imaginable: An equity-focused vision presents a picture of what equity embedded throughout the institution would look like yet is rooted in reality. It's easy to say that all policies, procedures, and behaviors will be approached with an equity lens, but is this realistic given the culture of the institution? The representational balance on the coalition team will help keep the reality factor in the conversation.

- Focused: An equity-focused vision should align with the institution's capacity yet be a stretch for the institution. The vision has to force a rethinking of behaviors. The coalition will need to consider the existing resources, resources available, and the infrastructure to accomplish the vision (Bailey et al., 2015).
- Strategic: An equity-focused vision should be simple. "Simplicity is essential" (Kotter, 2014, p. 79). A single-sentence vision statement, however, can be too abstract for people to react to, force people out of their comfort zone, and aim at being better where equity is concerned.

After considering the ground rules, the coalition should proceed with crafting the equity vision statement. Leaders will need to exhibit extreme patience and active listening during this process. Developing a vision takes time and usually will not be accomplished in one session. A great starting point is to review samples of good vision statements and break people into small groups to craft the vision. Each group should be facilitated by a champion. Using the principle of equity and the themes that have emerged, each group should craft a vision statement. The vision may be three to four sentences:

> It is our goal to become a high-performing institution focused on equity in the student and employee experience, resulting in greater retention of our students and employees. As we use the term *equity*, it refers to the fair practices and policies applied to each individual based on their needs. The term *experience* refers to how people move through the institution and the resulting perception. We want to create a welcoming environment rooted in equity that fosters a positive perspective of our institution.

The role of the coalition members and the college is evident in this sample implementation of the vision.

Once the coalition subgroups have crafted a sample vision statement, the small groups' vision statements should be shared with the larger group, and the coalition should respond to four critical questions in evaluating the strength of the vision statements:

1. How will an equity-focused vision affect our students?
2. How will an equity-focused vision affect our community and other partners?
3. How will an equity-focused vision affect our employees?
4. How do we know what data we will use to answer questions 1–3?

The answer to these questions will accomplish two things. First, the coalition can use this exercise to narrow down and refine an equity vision statement. Second, the responses to these questions keep the sense of urgency at the forefront of the vision. If there is not a dramatic effect resulting from the vision, then why move forward? Likely, the responses to these questions will have a dramatic response that will help the coalition in crafting and communicating the equity vision for the institution.

5

COMMUNICATE THE EQUITY VISION THROUGH INTENTIONAL COLLABORATION AND THE GOVERNANCE PROCESS

Chapter highlights: In this phase of becoming an equity-centered institution, we will share the elements of good communication of an equity-centered vision. The champions and EOT will have a specific function in communicating and refining the equity-vision through the governance structure.

Leadership focus areas: Organizational culture; governance, institutional policy, and legislation; institutional leadership; institutional infrastructure; communication; and collaboration.

E ffective communication is an essential leadership competency. Good communication throughout the institution is an essential tool to achieve strong working relationships among employees and working units. The importance of strong communication runs deep. Yet, many higher education institutions appear to have no strategic communication plan. Some leaders seem to believe that implementing equity programs and policies is the right thing to do, so stakeholders should just do it. Wrong! Higher education leaders must stop making general announcements about what they want to do. Rather, they must engage their stakeholders in planning and execution.

An equity vision, as critical as it is to the institution, cannot be provided in gigantic chunks; the information must be presented in simple form and easy to digest. In previous chapters of the book, we discussed important tools and strategies for the institution to employ to become an equity-centered institution. We explained how the senior leaders, champions, and the EOT must work collaboratively to craft an equity vision. Therefore, the work up to this point is still a draft. Until the entire institution has had an opportunity to weigh in on the vision, it is still a draft. In this chapter, we discuss how to use effective and broad communication strategies to move the draft equity vision to a final stage for implementation.

Characteristics of Effective Communication of the Equity Vision

Effective communication throughout the institution is an essential leadership competency that must be demonstrated to achieve strong working relationships among employees and working units of the institution. We encourage institutions to invest time into developing a strategic communication plan. Before the EOT begins to engage the broader college community in conversations about equity, they must be aware of the characteristics that will gain greater buy-in on the vision. When the equity vision is communicated across the college, key elements of transformational change must be incorporated into the communication process: defining the problem (equity), creating a sense of urgency (through data), and outlining the process thus far and the journey ahead for all groups. These components should be a part of what Kotter (2014) considers the successful elements of communicating vision:

- Simplicity: Given the complexity of what equity means, it's important to keep the communication of the vision simple. In this case, a visual of what equity means will probably ease immediate tension that can emerge from a sensitive topic (see Figure 1.1). The picture of the boys who can see the game and those who cannot demonstrates an understanding of equity with just one graphic.
- Metaphor, analogy, and example: People often relate to something familiar. If possible, draw an analogy or create an illustration that will make a connection for them. For example, in a presentation with a point regarding customer service, the following may be applicable: "Our student enrollment process should be less of a maze and more of a highway." This analogy is 15 words, and everyone will immediately relate to the scenario.
- Multiple forums: The forums for communication are important. In this chapter, we will address the intersection of leadership and utilizing the governance process. The way the message is delivered is often different for different groups. The senior leadership may be

looking at equity from one lens, while the governing board may be looking through another lens, and so on. The equity message, while similar, may be tweaked for each audience. The big takeaway here is to engage as many people as possible in the conversations about equity. In addition to the governance process, there are multiple mediums that can be used: newsletters, open forums, email blasts, other internal communication methods, or existing meetings.

- Repetition: Writing teachers are known for saying, "Introduce your main idea, elaborate on it, and summarize it in the end." As in the case of writing, repetition is necessary when communicating the equity vision. In this case, we recommend that institutions develop a strategic communication plan. Think about how people receive and absorb information. There may be different pieces to the communication plan depending on how the equity agenda is launched. However, aligning the communication with the goal and being consistent in the messaging will enhance the implementation flow along with the buy-in from constituent groups.

- Leadership by example: It is extremely critical for the senior leadership team and the coalition to model *leadership by example*. In the public forums and in the day-to-day interactions, people will be watching the leaders of the equity efforts. The senior leadership team and all coalition members will need to ensure that their behaviors are reflect the mission, vision, and core values of the institution and ensure that their behaviors are aligned with the equity vision. Any behavior exhibited outside of the vision can be used to sabotage the effort.

- Give-and-take: Institutional leadership behaviors are important throughout the transformation process, and these behaviors must be reflected in the communication process. We encourage leaders to practice active listening; this approach will help facilitators to "listen and be listened to" (Kotter, 2014, p. 101). Model good listening and others will likely listen to the message that is being communicated.

Since developing an equity vision may be new at most institutions, constituents must be able to understand the urgency of the change and see the possibilities for the future. Getting constituents to the point of understanding why change is taking place is no easy task when communicating the need for change. Communicating the need for change to different groups can compound the problem. We encourage leaders to reach out to constituent groups through the institution's established governance process. Why do we think this approach is helpful? Governance bodies typically consist of representatives who reflect the opinions of most stakeholders. Governance leaders, therefore, can be extended advocates for the effort and help with gaining buy-in from their constituent groups on becoming an equity-centered institution.

A Strategic, Comprehensive Plan for Communicating the Equity Vision

The primary goal of a communication strategy is to gain buy-in on the equity vision. The EOT must be willing to use the leadership competencies of active listening and transparency in this process. Active listening will create an opportunity for the coalition to receive input on the work completed. Transparency in the conversations will build trust throughout the organization, hence creating more buy-in on the equity vision. The process for achieving a final, college-wide approved vision means that the EOT must communicate, communicate, and communicate (Kotter, 2014). The approach must be both comprehensive and strategic. We offer a three-phased communication process that leads to a final, college-wide equity vision. Figure 5.1 illustrates the components of a comprehensive communication plan.

Communicate (Phase 1): Incorporating the Governance Structure to Communicate the Equity Vision

Similar to business and industry, higher education institutions have unique missions and visions that inform the public about how they propose to operate the institution. Most colleges and universities have some type of governance structure that allows faculty and staff to participate in major decisions concerning the operation of the college. In order to solicit input from faculty and staff, institutions create structures to create and disseminate information. It is for this reason that we encourage senior leaders, champions, and the EOT to use established governance structures to create and communicate the equity vision to the wider college community. Utilizing the governance structure will be the best approach to gaining the greatest momentum in communicating and advancing the equity vision.

Figure 5.1. Equity-centered communication process.

As Kotter (2014) suggests, the EOT should use multiple forums to communicate the vision. As practitioners in higher education, we suggest that the forum is guided by the governance structure and key stakeholder units within the institution. It's important to note that, depending on the institution, the executive leadership team and students may not be formally engaged in the governance process, but participation of these constituent groups is important to include in communicating and refining the vision. Column 1 in Table 5.1 highlights sample stakeholder units to embrace when communicating the equity vision. Column 2 shows the anticipated outcome for each stakeholder unit engagement session.

In each of the outcome sessions shown in Table 5.1, the majority of the membership of the equity oversight team (EOT) should have roles as presenters at the sessions so that people can see that everyone owns the equity vision. Implementing a transformational change such as "becoming an equity-centered institution" can be like walking a tightrope. Our observation is that walking

TABLE 5.1

Using the Governance Structure to Communicate and Refine the Equity Vision

Stakeholder Group	Outcome for the Session
Executive leadership team	Share input on the equity vision at a very transparent, somewhat granular level
	Gain more support at a level where resources will be determined
Faculty	Share input on the equity vision in a simplistic, digestible manner to inform the student and employee experience at the institution
Staff	Share input on the equity vision in a simplistic, digestible manner to inform the student and employee experience at the institution
Administrators	Share input on the equity vision to gain shared input on the feasibility of the vision
Students	Share input on the student experience where equity is concerned, which will further inform the vision
Board of trustees	Have a high-level feedback session or workshop designed to inform the Board on the equity concept and gain support for policies and resources that may be needed in the future.

a tightrope means that leaders must balance between the present and the proposed change, stepping very cautiously so as not to fall off the rope before the goal is accomplished. While moving forward cautiously, the champion(s) and EOT must create the culture of evidence among all constituent groups to develop a sense of urgency to act toward becoming an equity-centered institution. Creating a sense of urgency to launch an equity agenda does not detract from the great work that is already happening at the institution.

We recommend that a separate meeting be held with each constituent group—one session for faculty, another for staff, and another for administrators. The rationale for this approach is that the messaging and responses may be slightly different for each group. Since many of the conversations surrounding equity focus on academic achievement disparities among students of color and other learners, the lenses (views) of faculty regarding equity may be a sensitive conversation. Consequently, faculty may push back on the data being presented about learning outcomes' inequities. Staff and administrators may not have those same concerns.

To remain in control of the time and purpose of the conversation, separate forums are typically more effective than combined sessions. Here's another tip: Consider using existing forums that are already in place to host college-wide conversations at the college. If the facilitators of the existing forums can host the equity conversations as a part of existing meetings/structures, people may not feel like they are being called to "another" meeting. For faculty, the structure may be a faculty senate meeting. At multi-college institutions, this may call for more than one presentation. For student services, there may be "dedicated time" identified for stakeholders to catch up on case management or other projects that bring the student services units together as a group.

Throughout this communication process, practicing strong communication leadership skills will be critical to getting to a successful outcome. It's important to remember to be transparent and confident, to listen actively, to be consistent, and to be an advocate for the equity vision. Listen carefully for barriers that emerge in the conversation. During the conversations with constituent groups, don't try to address the barriers; just listen to the perspectives of the participants.

Investing time to meet separately with each constituent group is likely to garner a lot of respect from your internal stakeholders. We recommend the following approach for conducting the discussion groups with stakeholders.

Executive Leadership

The executive leadership should be consulted twice: the first time for shared input on the equity vision, the second conversation to focus on resources needed to support the broadly accepted equity vision. During this initial meeting, the executive champion and other champions should plan to make a presentation to the executive leadership team. The presentation should include the following:

1. Sense of urgency statement: Provide a detailed update on the work of the EOT. Share the data collected (qualitative and quantitative) at all phases in a slightly sophisticated but not so granular way.
2. Engagement plan: Outline the progress and steps taken to advance the equity agenda and those constituent groups engaged in various conversations. Share a simple timeline for the next steps in the process.
3. Shared vision: Present the EOT's shared equity vision statement, gauge the executive leadership interest, and solicit feedback.
4. Next steps: Once the champion has provided an update on the work of the EOT, the next steps for the EOT must be explained. The champion must be prepared to discuss how the equity team plans to move forward with the equity work at the college. The champion must be able to discuss the work of the coalition so that the executive team will be able to understand the equity-related issues at the college. Until the executive leadership understands the issues, the EOT will not be able to take the next step toward "becoming an equity-centered institution."

Also, in the conversation with the executive leadership team, the champions should be open to input, especially regarding the barriers to success the executive leadership may anticipate. The goal is to keep the executive leadership team informed and motivated to continue supporting transformational change. This can be an "in your face respectfully" session—real talk where the environment fosters and supports disagreements and open exchange of perspectives. Present the data and be transparent and candid about the results. It's okay for the executive champion to provide an opinion. In fact, since the role of the champion has been explained to the other members of the team, the executives may expect the champion to provide insight about what is going on—that's why there is a champion!

Faculty

The agenda for the faculty forum is similar to the presentation to the executive leadership team, but the material should be presented differently, focusing on issues of interest to faculty. The forum should include the following elements:

1. Sense of urgency: Share the data collected (qualitative and quantitative) at all phases in a slightly sophisticated but a faculty-oriented way.
2. Engagement plan: Outline the steps taken so far and the people engaged in the process. Provide a simple timeline. Conduct a brief dialogue session regarding the faculty's impression of the student and faculty experience from an equity perspective.
3. Shared vision: Present the EOT's shared vision draft and gauge faculty reaction.
4. Next steps: Once the champion has provided an update on the work of the EOT, the next steps for the EOT must be explained. The champion must be prepared to discuss how the equity team plans to move forward with the equity work at the college. The champion must be able to discuss the work of the coalition so that the executive team will be able to understand the equity-related issues at the college. Until the faculty as a group understands the issues, the coalition will not be effective with moving forward toward "becoming an equity-centered institution."

In many faculty governance structures, there may be an executive committee. If so, it is a good idea to present the equity draft vision information to the executive committee first. Working with the executive committee first may provide insight into how effective the presentation will be to the larger group of faculty representatives. The executive committee may also have suggestions on when and how to present the material to the wider faculty community. For example, at multi-campus institutions, there may be an existing campus-based faculty senate meeting. Getting on the agenda of an existing meeting can be helpful so that people do not feel like they are being forced to attend another meeting.

Staff

In some workplace settings, staff members do not have as much access to information as other units within the organization. Some staff members may fear that a big transformational change will result in their role being eliminated or reduced (McPhail, 2016). From the staff members' perspective, a transformational change such as equity can be viewed as detrimental to their role in the organization. Consequently, for this group, more than any other, the presentation should illustrate the WIFM (what's in it for me?). Staff members' lack of understanding about the reasons behind the equity effort can be detrimental to the process.

Senior leaders, champions, and coalition members leading the equity efforts must use the discussion forums with staff to explain the equity work and why their roles are important to helping the college become more equity centered. In our experience as practitioners in higher education, the staff may be very supportive of impactful initiatives, but they need to see how their roles fit with the new directions. The staff forum should include the following:

1. Sense of urgency: Share the data collected (qualitative and quantitative) at all phases presented in a simplistic way.
2. Engagement plan: Outline the steps that have been taken to advance the equity agenda. In addition, it is a good idea to identify the individuals who are engaged in implementing the equity work. The engagement plan should be illustrated in a simple format to demonstrate how the equity work is progressing at the institution. The leaders of the equity agenda should create opportunities to engage stakeholders in brief dialogue sessions to collect feedback regarding their impression of how students and faculty are experiencing the college's efforts to advance the equity agenda.
3. Shared vision: Present the coalition's shared vision draft, gauge their reaction, and encourage feedback.
4. Next steps: Once the champion has provided an update on the work of the EOT, the next steps for the EOT must be explained. The champion must be prepared to discuss how the equity team plans to move forward with the equity work at the college. The champion must be able to discuss the work of the EOT so that the staff will be able to understand the equity-related issues. The EOT should take the time to ensure that staff members understand the issues surrounding equity before moving forward with full execution of the equity plans.

The most important element that will emerge is the practicality of this equity vision with the staff. If the staff cannot embrace the equity vision, the chances are the ideas have not been presented in practical enough terms for them to see how it is aligned with the work they do on a day-to-day basis.

Administrators

In this book, the term *administrators* refer to anyone below the executive leadership level (presidents) but above the staff level. The forum with administrators is extremely important to gaining feedback about the feasibility of the equity vision. The forum with the administrators should focus on the following:

1. Sense of urgency: Share the data collected (qualitative and quantitative) at all phases in a sophisticated, transparent way.

2. Engagement plan: Outline the steps that have been taken to advance the equity agenda. In addition, it is a good idea to identify the individuals who are engaged in implementing the equity work. The engagement plan should be illustrated in a simple format to demonstrate how the equity work is progressing at the institution. The leaders of the equity agenda should create opportunities to engage stakeholders in brief dialogue sessions to collect feedback regarding their impression of how students and faculty are experiencing the college's efforts to advance the equity agenda.

3. Shared vision: Present the coalition's shared vision draft and gauge their reaction.

4. Next steps: Once the champion has provided an update on the work of the EOT to the administrators, the next steps for the EOT must be explained. The champion must be prepared to discuss how the equity team plans to move forward with the equity work at the college. The champion must be able to discuss the work of the EOT so that the administrators will be able to understand the equity-related issues. Since the administrators at all levels of the institution will be responsible for helping to implement equity programming, it is important for them to understand the issues related to advancing the equity agenda. The EOT must ensure that administrators are ready to accept the equity plan before taking the next step in becoming an equity-centered leader centered institution.

In addition to students, the richest input will probably come from this administrative group. The administrators are "on the ground" with the students and staff-level employees; they have a real sense of what will and will not work. Midlevel managers and administrators are often overlooked when implementing transformational change initiatives such as becoming an equity-centered institution. According to Anicich and Hirsh (2017b), individuals in middle-power states have a bidirectional (i.e., unstable) vertical orientation, reflecting the subjective perception that their power is neither consistently higher nor lower than the power of others in their social network. The influence of this group can be leveraged in the implementation stage if trust is garnered on the front end. A good reason to engage midlevel leaders in the transformational change process is the opportunity to use their skills to help interpret the mind-set of the people on the front lines. Midlevel leaders serve a key role in implementing change in hierarchical institutions by exerting influence in upward and downward directions (Floyd & Wooldridge, 1992).

Board of Trustees
It is essential for the president to keep the board of trustees informed about how key issues such as equity impact the institution. Appropriately informing

the board, especially in the early stages of the equity efforts, can make a huge difference between success and failure of the institution's effort to become more equity centered. For the board of trustees, the goal of the equity conversation should be to provide an update on the progress of the equity work and to keep the board engaged at a high level regarding the equity agenda. The conversation with the board can be conducted in a process similar to what happens during budget season, such as board workshop or at board retreats. Institutions are encouraged to use equity discussion as an opportunity to educate the board and update them on the future of the institution where equity is concerned. Since one of the board's governance responsibilities includes adopting a vision statement for the college, we encourage leaders to engage the board in the development of the equity vision statement for the institution. The degree of board of engagement will generally depend on the size and complexity of the organization and the overall culture of board engagement at the institution.

As stated in chapter 4, it is important to align the equity vision with the college's vision. Bear in mind that the board is the body that will approve the resources needed to support the equity agenda; they should be kept informed throughout the equity change process.

Student Forums
Kay McClenney (2016), the former director of Community College Survey of Student Engagement (CCSSE), coined the phrase "students don't do optional." Higher education leaders must remember this phrase when they plan events to engage students. Today's students face significant competing demands for their time. So, attracting their attention to get them to come to a forum to discuss equity will require more than a simple invitation. Realize that there will need to be some type of incentive for students to attend meetings. Community college students are very transient, work, and some are caretakers and have children. Their time is extremely valuable, and the information received from them will be equally as valuable as other stakeholders in designing the equity agenda for the college. While the content of the student forums can be the same as employees, we encourage leaders to tailor the delivery of the student forum to fit the needs of students. The following list provides some suggestions for conducting meetings with students:

1. Sense of urgency: Explain to students how the equity agenda is designed to improve the student experience at the college. Share the data collected (qualitative and quantitative) at all phases in a very simplistic format.
2. Engagement plan: Create a brief, student-friendly dialogue regarding their impression of the student experience from an equity perspective.

3. Shared vision: Present the EOT's shared vision statement draft and gauge their reaction. Be sure to draw connections to the student experience.

Institutions may want to allow students to describe their experiences at the institution from entry to exit. When institutional data is shared with students, we recommend the use of student-friendly infographics that focus the conversation on the students' perspectives of their experiences. The intent of this type of dialogue with students is to create an environment where students can feel comfortable during the discussion.

Also, rely on a give-and-take strategy in the discussion with the student group. The EOT member leading the conversation should use an informal approach and even dress informally so that students will be more likely to relax and participate in the conversation. The session with students can be treated like a focus group where students can be asked to respond to open-ended questions on the topic of equity. It is important to let the conversation flow while encouraging all participants to be fully engaged in the conversation. When engaging students, it is a good idea to limit interjections and attempts to solve the problems expressed—allow the students to offer suggestions for how to solve the equity issues. The difficult task will be to keep the conversation focused on equity and not allow the discussion to morph into a complaint session about parking or the bookstore—most leaders already know that students are not happy about either.

Communicate (Phase 2): Reconvene the EOT to Finalize the Equity Vision and Validate Input

After speaking with each internal stakeholder group, the EOT will need to regroup to synthesize and validate input received from the various forums. The EOT members should ask, "Did we learn anything new that was not considered in the draft equity vision statement?" If so, the team should consider the new information, which can be used to enhance the equity vision for the college. After considering all input, the EOT should finalize the equity vision statement and prepare to circle back to meet with the internal stakeholders.

Communicate (Phase 3): Circle Back to Share the Final, College-Wide Vision

This last phase of the development of the communication plan is often discounted and is probably the most important element. The EOT must communicate the final equity vision to the college community. If the greater college community can see their input incorporated in the final equity vision statement, they are more likely to support it in the long term. The vision statement should be presented in a user-friendly manner. For example, illustrations of input can be presented using a different color font to highlight the change and input received. The following statement was the draft equity statement developed by a community college in the Midwest:

> It is our goal to become a high-performing institution focused on equity in the student and employee experience, resulting in greater retention of our students and employees. As we use this term *equity*, it refers to the fair practices and policies applied to each individual based on their needs. The term *experience* refers to how people move through the institution and the resulting perception. We want to create a welcoming environment rooted in equity that fosters a positive perspective of our institution.

After considering all of the input, the college revised its equity statement:

> It is our goal to become a high-performing institution focused on an equitable experience for anyone attending, working, or visiting any of our campuses. As we use this term *equity*, it refers to the fair practices and policies applied to each individual based on their needs. The term *experience* refers to how people move through the institution and the resulting perception. We want to create a welcoming environment rooted in equity that fosters a positive perspective of our institution internally and externally.

The final, college-wide vision statement should be sent to all internal stakeholders, perhaps electronically, or consider making the announcement of the vision statement a special event such as a college-wide meeting. Strive to link the equity work with the college's mission, vision, and strategic plan. This approach will ensure that all constituent groups understand that equity is embedded in the culture of the college. It will be important to thank everyone who participated in the forums and highlight the changes that emerged from those forums. The transparent courageous conversations highlighted in this section are necessary to communicate the vision for developing a culture that embraces equity throughout the college.

Finally, once the communication plan is in place, it is important to keep the momentum going. It is key to the success of the equity agenda. To keep the momentum gained from the equity forums, senior leaders, champions, and the coalition should strive to anticipate the unexpected by building on the data collected. Senior leaders must strive to foster an environment that empowers all stakeholders to embrace this equity vision that will propel the college further toward becoming an equity-centered institution.

With a considerable amount of preliminary work completed, it is time to reconvene the coalition team to debrief and prepare to triangulate data and determine the next steps to advance the equity efforts.

6

UTILIZE INSTITUTIONAL LEADERSHIP AND COLLABORATION TO EMPOWER EMPLOYEES INTO BROAD-BASED ACTION

Chapter highlights: In this chapter, the focus is on types of equity barriers, the removal of equity barriers, and barrier removal management.

Leadership focus areas: Institutional leadership, advocacy, mobilizing others, fundraising and relationship cultivation, communication, and collaboration.

As the equity transformation continues to evolve, so will the identification of the barriers. Our experiences have taught us that through the process of communicating the vision (as highlighted in chapter 4), barriers to equity usually emerge during this stage of the equity work. Specifically, the communication plan helps the EOT identify aspects of the infrastructure that may unintentionally nurture barriers. After the barriers have been addressed, it is necessary to create a structure where the coalition feels empowered to identify and make recommendations to manage the elimination of the barriers that are blocking the equity work at the college.

Types of Equity Barriers

While many specific examples of equity barriers may surface in the various groups participating in open forums, it is important to spend quality time analyzing the barriers. When all data are collected and synthesized, the barriers, typically, fall into three distinct categories: people, structures, and systems. Some people will not embrace an equity vision. In some cases, the cultural landscape of the region prevents people from being able to see the need for equity. Unfortunately, many areas throughout the United States still struggle with equality and are just getting to the point of examining the equity concept. Many organization cultures are entrenched in norms that prevent equity from evolving to the forefront of a college's operations. On the other hand, there are people who simply resist any type of change. In cases where there is resistance to change, some individuals may dig their heels and make every attempt to sabotage the effort to move the equity agenda forward. The last type of person is likely to present a challenge to the equity work at the college. This person may demonstrate the behavior of coming to work, doing a job, and not concerning themselves with anything that may cause a change in their roles.

The second equity barrier in community colleges is organizational structure. This is evident in most institutions but especially in large, multi-campus community colleges. According to McPhail (2016), traditional organizational, hierarchical community college structures influence the delivery of programs and services. McPhail (2016) stated, "The capacity to implement programs and services that require multiple, simultaneous management capabilities is well beyond the traditional bureaucratic organizational structures and cultures operating in most community colleges" (p. 57).

Moreover, organizational structures can prevent an equity agenda from moving forward. In many cases, structural limitations are unintentional barriers that do not emerge until an equity-centered vision is put in place at the institution. In an article entitled "Pathways to Completion: Guidelines to Boosting Student Success," Terry O'Banion (2011) said,

> The historical architecture of education that the community colleges adopted from four-year colleges and universities encourages "silos" that discourage collaboration: faculty members divide into departments around disciplines; staff in student affairs and academic affairs barely communicate on some campuses; the curriculum is chopped into career/technical education and liberal arts/transfer education. This entrenched structure has not gone unnoticed. (p. 9)

An example of how organizational structures may serve as a barrier to equity in an employment situation is illustrated in the following scenario:

> The EOT has learned that the onboarding process for new employees at a large multi-campus institution was unpleasant and not welcoming, especially to some groups of people attending these sessions. The information

in the presentation and language included in the "script" of the facilitator were not equitably conducted. After the EOT explored this barrier, it was determined that the problem was the organizational structure of the Human Resources office. The division was so decentralized that the resources were inconsistent and fragmented. In this case, there was a human resource generalist at each campus. Each generalist used a different script, placing their own views of the college and people in that script. In addition, there was not one common presentation, and the photos at one orientation only included White middle-aged people. Not much diversity there.

Structures like the one portrayed in this scenario can make or break broad-based engagement of stakeholders in the college's equity effort.

The last type of barrier is the systemic barrier. Systemic barriers are more complex and more difficult to resolve because they are not readily visible. Feagin (2006) developed a theory of systemic racism to interpret the highly racialized character and development of society. Systemic barriers can be found when practices or policies are put in place that discriminate against individuals by screening them out from participation—that's an inequity. Systemic barriers are often an unintentional consequence, especially where technology is concerned. Community colleges across America are working hard to meet students where they are to provide equitable services. Archaic enrollment systems can be a barrier to achieving this goal. For example, there are only three large student information systems available to most community colleges: Banner, PeopleSoft, and Jenzabar. There are also new "products" that can help colleges identify students' needs: Are they working while attending college? Are they the first in their family to attend college? These are all factors that influence a student's success and if addressed with appropriate support practices create opportunities to provide equitable services.

However, in many cases, large, complex student information systems are designed in a way that makes integration of specific support services or intervention in the technological infrastructure extremely difficult to implement. Meanwhile, institutions enroll students without being able to collect essential information from them that would likely increase their success. Systemic barriers are also intertwined with organizational culture. Some systems have been in place too long and serve as barriers to students and employees. Leaders must foster an equity-centered organizational culture while the transformational change process is unfolding. Sometimes existing systems at the institution create a culture that makes it difficult to align an equity vision with college's mission and the core values of the institution.

Whether it's people, structure, or systems, these barriers act as the *lid*. Maxwell (2007) describes the lid in reference to an individual's leadership ability. We argue that the lid can extend beyond the individual to the institution's culture. Therefore, we advance an alternative definition, "the leadership ability [of everyone at the institution] is the lid that determines [the institution's] effectiveness. The lower an [institution's] ability to lead, the lower the lid on [the institution's] potential" (Maxwell, 2014, p. 1). The people, systems, and structures create the lid. Further, the people often make the lid lower than it needs to be by saying, "We have always done it that way." To move an equity vision forward, it will take the AACC (2018) leadership competencies such as institutional leadership; mobilizing other communications; and advocating collaboration, resource management, and supportive team building to help people raise the lid and remove barriers.

Removing Equity Barriers

Removing barriers must be an important part of the equity goal when implementing transformational change. However, goals are exactly that—something to strive for. We use the phrase *removing barriers* because it is important to strive to totally remove them, and in some cases that may be a realistic expectation; however, in other situations, leaders may only be able to reduce barriers. Reducing barriers can still provide the momentum needed to execute the equity vision.

The path to removing barriers to equity relies heavily on institutional leadership competencies and behaviors. When evaluating the challenges with people, structure, and systems that serve as barriers to an equity vision, the EOT will need to work together to position the college for the future. It is important for the EOT to be consistent in their communication and actions as they move forward. Kotter (2014) suggests specific strategies when people, structure, and system barriers emerge. In this book, we aligned the change strategies with the AACC (2018) competencies for community college leaders. Table 6.1 shows the leadership competency and behavior required to remove barriers to the equity vision.

Given that people (attitude and behaviors) can be a barrier to an equity vision, the EOT and CEO of the college must understand the strategies that can eliminate or reduce barriers. The people are the core of advancing the equity vision; the CEO and coalition should focus on developing a training plan in advance of communicating the plan and be prepared to implement the training phase of the change process. Training designed to foster a culture of equity has many components where the right leadership behaviors will be important.

There are many different types of equity training models offered in higher education: identity in the workplace, understanding privilege, power in the workplace, unconscious bias, and so on. The EOT will have to determine which aspects of traditionally offered training will be included in the institution's work. The following are steps the EOT can take in beginning the implementation process for advancing equity.

First, the EOT and administration will need to continue supporting teamwork at the institution. Relationships take time to develop, and in an institution where equity is not at the center of the mission and vision it will require strong commitment from the leadership team to move the equity agenda forward. Members of the EOT should use team-building activities to create a focused equity initiative. Training activities can be developed around case studies, interactive activities, or role-play. For faculty training, consider using scenarios and activities that mirror the classroom. Regardless of the audience, institutions are encouraged to simulate real aspects of employees' current responsibilities in the training activities. If possible, strive to integrate equity training activities into existing meetings, events, or activities. One of biggest pushbacks in equity-based team-building activities is equity training being viewed as *another activity that distracts employees from doing their work.*

Second, the EOT and senior administration will need to ensure there is an effective performance management system in place. When equity-minded practices are the expectation for all employees, institutions can link employee performance to the attainment of equity goals. How do equity-minded practices work? Supervisors and employees identify goals that are aligned with the equity vision.

Third, the EOT and administration will need to continue to advocate and locate professional development opportunities that align with implementing the equity vision. In higher education, while there are many professional development activities, very few are focused on equity. Many colleges have a justification process for requesting professional development funding. What if one requirement for the funding was "Describe how this professional development funding will advance the equity agenda at our college"? By connecting the equity efforts to funding, the institution will begin to encourage people to think about equity and how it can connect to the institution's equity vision. Further, the accountability system must include a method for the employees to share information after they engage in professional development workshops or conferences. By sharing information and continuing to conduct bold, courageous conversations, a new culture of promising practices can emerge.

The barrier removal process would be incomplete without a close examination of structural barriers. Unlike dealing with the personnel, structural barriers are likely to be less challenging to address and more likely to be within the CEO and leadership team's span of control. The EOT should partner with the CEO and administration to hold collaborative conversations about structural issues that may interfere with the equity agenda. Structural barriers are usually identified through the process of developing the communication plan. The EOT should identify those barriers and seek to identify the factors that created the problem. Typically, the EOT is not expected to facilitate structural change, which is the reason for the collaboration with the CEO.

When a transformation takes place, the structural inequities have the potential to undermine the vision (Kotter, 2014). Take time to identify the silos, centralized or decentralized constructs, or unit structures that may prevent an equity vision from moving forward. The CEO and leadership team must create a forum for the EOT to share information obtained about the structural barriers from the open forums. At this stage in the change process, it will be important for the executive leadership team to devise a plan to reduce or eliminate those structural challenges. And, the plan of action to remove the barriers must be communicated to all constituent groups.

Finally, the equity vision must be aligned with the institution's policies and practices. When the evaluation of the systemic barriers takes place, some overlapping barriers are usually identified. Earlier in this section, we advanced the idea that a thorough evaluation process can potentially reduce people's resistance to change. Unfortunately, many institutions frequently skip the evaluation process. At many institutions, the evaluation process is a perfect example of a practice that can stand some improvement; no system is perfect. Most CEOs have the desire to create a system that will create a sense of accountability around the vision, but processes, like an evaluation process, are also rooted in the culture of the organization. Institutions must develop methods to conduct an effective evaluation of relevant policies and practices. The evaluation process will examine the extent to which equity principles are embedded in the organization's culture. When a program rises to the systemic level, it is very entrenched in the culture. Once systemic change is under way, people often feel overwhelmed by the magnitude of the task. When the culture shifts in this direction, the EOT will be extremely valuable in this process by continuing to be advocates and influencers who can support the cultural change of imbedding equity into policies and practices.

Table 6.1 illustrates types of barriers, corrective strategies, and the leadership competency and behaviors expected to remove barriers.

Removing barriers is usually the most time consuming and difficult part of this phase of the equity work. However, any time barriers are removed, the

TABLE 6.1
Barrier and Leadership Competency Matrix

The Barrier	The Strategy	The Leadership Competency	The Leadership Behavior
People	Training	Support team building Institutional leadership Collaboration Communication	Nurture relationships to continue to build support for the equity vision
		Performance management Institutional leadership Advocacy and mobilizing others Communication	Ensure systems for accountability and performance management are in place to support the equity vision
		Advocate for professional development	Align professional development activities with the equity vision
Structures	Ensure compatibility with the equity vision	Problem-solving techniques Institutional infrastructure:	Seek to identify what factors contribute to the faulty structure and use resources to implement a solution that supports the equity vision

results must be managed and maintained. The same is true for monitoring and managing equity barriers.

Barrier Removal Management

We believe that barrier removal management is a skill that all leaders need to possess when it comes to advancing the equity agenda. The key to managing barriers is to remain consistent. The guiding coalition and administration's role will now shift to inspect what you expect. In other words, the administrator will begin to incorporate accountability into their implementation of the equity vision. When behaviors contrary to the equity vision emerge, continue to evaluate if those behaviors fall into the category of people, structures, or systems. Then, determine if there is already a solution in place. If not, revisit the strategy outlined in the previous section of this chapter. If the barrier has been identified, and a solution is in place, hold everyone whose behaviors are not aligned with the equity vision accountable. Over time, people will begin to understand the expectation, but embedding account-ability throughout the institution is an ever-evolving process.

As an institution strives to implement an equity agenda, the infrastructure must be in place to support the inevitable behavioral change that will need to occur with the people. We encourage senior leaders to be mindful that individual or group attitudes and behaviors can serve as a barrier in the change process. This type of barrier impacts equity efforts on all levels. When the people, systems, and structures are aligned with the vision, the coalition and others will be empowered to manage and ensure that barriers do not return.

7

GENERATE SHORT-TERM WINS THROUGH RELATIONSHIP CULTIVATION

Chapter highlights: In this chapter, the discussion focuses on characteristics of short-term wins, the role of short-term wins in the equity agenda, planning for short-term wins, and the role of leadership in fostering and reporting short-term wins.

Leadership focus areas: Institutional leadership, institutional infrastructure, advocacy, mobilizing others, fundraising and relationship cultivation, communications, and collaboration.

Maxwell (2004) often suggests that the key to leadership is influence. He argues that influence is an important component in leadership because it creates *followership*—a term one of the authors, Kimberly Beatty, coined to explain how people line up and support their leaders. When followership occurs around an issue, people begin to follow the vision because they now can *see others engaged in the process too.* To maintain momentum, especially where equity is concerned, the coalition and leadership of the college can leverage the followership to demonstrate short-term wins, not only once but throughout the equity transformation.

Characteristics of Short-Term Equity Wins

Becoming an equity-centered higher education institution will not happen without leaders recognizing short-term wins. Short-term wins are "visible; as a result, people can see for themselves whether the result is real or just hype" (Kotter, 2014, p. 126). We encourage institutions to accurately report on the progress; do not exaggerate results. Let's revisit the discussion on the *sense of urgency* and the type of challenges encountered in a community college environment where equity is concerned. We recommended using the institution's data to display the gaps in equitable student achievement or using data regarding the gender and ethnic make-up of the workplace to illustrate representational disparities. When demonstrating short-term wins, the EOT and administration should go back to the data and show the results—what has improved or changed? For example, many states are using performance measures to reduce achievement gaps. At one institution in the Midwest, those achievement gaps created an equity challenge for the higher education institution. Just recently at the faculty convocation at one of the colleges in the state, the CEO shared the latest data—the college moved the needle toward closing achievement gaps by 2% in high-impact academic areas. What has the CEO accomplished by taking this action? First, there was a broad-based audience, so everyone was able to celebrate the accomplishment. Second, the CEO created momentum by demonstrating progress (short-term win). Third, the faculty are the most influential group in any college, and unveiling a short-term win to this group helped encourage them to support the equity work to continue to gain momentum.

Also, short-term wins should be "unambiguous—there can be little argument" over the win presented (Kotter, 2014, p. 126). In essence, the short-term win must be concrete. The example of the CEO showing the data is a perfect illustration because, while people will try, it is difficult to argue with the data.

Another example of a transparent short-term win is a process or policy that has been changed that yields positive results. There's a community college in the Southwest that had allowed their policies to become outdated. This deficit in efficiency prevented critical processes from moving forward in a timely fashion and ultimately negatively impacted classroom practices. For example, the hiring policies were too vague, and the procedures associated with it were equally vague. As a result, the employee search process often varied depending on who was chairing the search, and the results were always the same—an internal candidate was selected. What are we suggesting here? It's great to have a culture that supports and grooms its own to progress through the institution, but if there is already a lack of equity and diversity in the ranks, the employee demographics will not change. Through the governance process, the procedure and policy were rewritten at this institution. Now, there is a consistent process that yields a diverse group of finalists equitably across all categories (age, gender, race, and affiliation). The CEO now has transparent results to communicate broadly to the college. More importantly, with fair and equitable employment processes, the faculty and staff can start to mirror the community they serve.

Short-term wins must also be "clearly related to the change effort" (Kotter, 2014, p. 126). Equity must remain at the center of the short-term win. Remember, the transformation is focused on the vision of becoming an equity-centered institution, which, in the end, should impact the student and employee experience. The previous examples, closing equity gaps and hiring diverse faculty, are directly linked to the equity vision. It's important that the CEO and EOT routinely connect their messages to the equity vision or the vision will get lost in the celebration. For a transformation of this magnitude to maintain its momentum, repetition and consistency are important. Keeping the messaging consistent whether communicating internally or externally will help gain trust and more buy-in for the equity vision.

The EOT and CEO will need to use the broadest forums possible to communicate the equity vision. Using existing forums such as faculty convocation, in-service programs or professional development days for all employees, and other existing gatherings are excellent ways to communicate with stakeholders. If there are existing social media or electronic platforms at the college, use those to communicate the equity wins. For example, a large multi-campus college in the Mid-Atlantic region routinely uses an electronic newsletter to keep stakeholders informed about the college's progress with the equity initiatives. The accomplishments of the equity team are listed on the website and updated on a regular basis. The leader of the equity team at a college in California developed an electronic student success newsletter that is distributed once per semester. The updates on equity milestones are included in the student success newsletter. Without the communication of short-term wins, the equity vision may appear to be a fad that has passed.

The Role of Short-Term Equity Wins

Now that the characteristics of short-term equity wins have been described, it is also important to emphasize the role of short-term equity wins. Why is this important? Short-term equity wins can "provide the evidence that sacrifices are worth it" (Kotter, 2014, p. 127). Providing data and/or other forms of tangible results can provide justification for the equity transformation. We shouldn't have to provide justification, but the reality is that people will more likely embrace the equity agenda when they see positive results.

Also, displaying short-term wins in an equity transformation can serve as a reward, especially for the EOT. At this point, the team has put their hearts and souls into the equity vision, probably facing a lot of conflict from different stakeholder groups. Celebrating the short-term win will be received as a reward for their hard work. The EOT can see that their leadership was not in vain. The coalition will continue to feel empowered and motivated to push the vision forward.

In this phase of the transformation process, there is an opportunity to fine-tune the vision statement and/or strategies as necessary. Short-term wins can spark celebration and conversation that may lead to modifications in policies and practices. When the equity results and the journey to achieving them are presented to different groups, the EOT has an opportunity to rethink the approach based on the response from the college community. For example, let's return to the hiring procedure changes and the results presented given the change in process. What if the college community had not gotten excited about the idea that more diverse populations needed to be hired? Maybe they are not thrilled that an equity-minded process is being applied because it reduces the committee's previous autonomy for selecting their favorite candidate for the job. If this is the case, there is an opportunity to revisit the strategies and, more importantly, how those strategies are communicated to the wider community. Essentially, communicating the short-term equity wins should create a learning opportunity for the EOT as it continues to present equity wins because there will be additional opportunities to move the equity agenda forward.

Celebrating short-term equity wins can also "undermine cynics and self-serving resisters" (Kotter, 2014, p. 127). Especially with an equity agenda, we acknowledge that there will be detractors along the way. Remember, equity is a topic that not only forces people to look at the institution but also requires individuals to examine themselves and their attitudes and values differently—there's a deep examination at the individual, unit, and organization level. Many people may not want to make that investment or may not want to face the realities that will emerge if they conduct the self-examination. People in this category may come around to see the value of the equity vision when the self-examination is complete. This means that campus leaders will need to use the competency of mobilizing others. Communicating short-term wins may, in this case, serve to convert people who are still on the fence. Clear communication and continued advocacy for the equity vision may stifle objectors because it is difficult for detractors to argue with the evidence. Concrete short-term equity wins can create an evidentiary trail of success.

We have observed that the most difficult level of the organization to keep engaged appears to the mid-level leaders. The location of mid-level leaders in the organization's architecture creates communication barriers (Beatty, 2011). These communication barriers exist because these administrators are sometimes unable to access information in a format they can use. Short-term equity wins can serve as a motivator to keep this group engaged. Mid-level leaders are often the individuals in an organization charged with the tough task of implementing something without being able to see real results in a timely manner. Remember, members of this layer of the organization are represented on the EOT; their membership, coupled with the demonstrated results supporting the equity vision, will boost their leadership capacity and sometimes their credibility with staff. Again, it goes back to followership. It is difficult to get the mid-level leaders on board given the multiple operational tasks they have, and it is especially hard for managers to get their people on board. Short-term wins will give everyone confidence. Likely, after one round of short-term wins, more managers will be on board with the equity vision, and it will only increase after each round of presentations. The credibility of this group will continue to rise.

During the equity planning process, mid-level leaders routinely get exposed to real-life ethical dilemmas and solutions. During this component of the equity process, mid-level leaders should be introduced to strategies that help them gain an understanding of their effectiveness as leaders. This exercise might take the form of asking each leader to develop a personal perspective of what equity means to their department or unit. This statement can form the basis by which leaders make decisions; employees assess ethical dilemmas and where an organization's equity vision is put into practice.

Mid-level leaders should be expected to enhance their knowledge of how to apply equity in the workplace to enable personal growth. Engagement in this level of planning also helps the mid-level leader establish the balance between their values and the stated values of the institution.

The final outcome of communicating short-term equity wins is to continue to build momentum and excitement for the equity vision. Those who were neutral about equity will become supporters; those who were inactive will become active (Kotter, 2014). People will no longer be able to argue with results. With the champions, EOT, and CEO exhibiting all the institutional competencies of transparency and advocacy for the vision, the organization will become energized around embedding equity in the culture of the institution.

Planning for Short-Term Equity Wins

Often when leaders are in the heat of the transformational change, they do not take the time to plan for short-term wins. Instead, they end up praying for the wins (Kotter, 2014). Good strategy development requires planning for victories, which requires vision. Vision should emerge from the CEO and be implemented by the EOT and the managers. When leading an equity transformation, the plan for the victories must originate from the top. The advocacy for the equity vision must never cease; otherwise, the college community will lose confidence in the vision. Within that vision, CEOs should anticipate the wins that will occur and admit when they don't. For example, if the data reflecting an impact on closing achievement gaps has not occurred, it is still important to share the data and state, "We had hoped/planned to see better progress, but we will continue to press forward." People need to see that there is a plan for progress.

The other part of planning for equity wins is the timing of those wins. Organizations that do not plan for wins over a period of time will not succeed with the transformation (Kotter, 2014). In the case of an equity transformation, you need two to three short-term wins. A complete equity transformation is going to take 3 to 5 years. Short-term wins should be planned at 14 and 24 months minimally (Kotter, 2014). Another win could be planned for the 36-month timeframe. This way, momentum is maintained and there is a better chance of the equity vision being integrated into the fabric of the institution. Becoming a equity centered is not a quick fix—it is a step by step journey.

Role of Leadership and Management

Throughout this text, we have been talking about the leadership competencies required to lead an equity transformation; however, management is also very important, especially in this phase of delivering short-term wins. As described in an earlier section, the leadership team should plan for the wins, which also includes supporting the strategies in the budgeting process. The leadership should systematically target objectives and budget for them (Kotter, 2014). The management, on the other hand, will continue to create plans and organize for the implementation that leads to short-term wins. It's important that both are leveraged in this process. As we move to the last phases of the equity transformation, leadership (vision) and management (implementers) need to be in sync to maintain momentum and infuse equity throughout the institution. The relationship between leadership and management make short-term results possible and can lead to a highly successful equity transformation.

The Integration of Short-Term Wins Into Goals and Objectives

The institution's commitment to communicating the short-term wins of its equity work must be balanced and integrated in all of its ongoing programs and services—providing evidence that progress is taking place. Signs of progress with the equity work must be visible to students, faculty, administrators, those already in the system, and those not yet engaged. In equity-centered institutions, equity issues are evaluated continuously and should be reported to the campus constituent groups. Because of the fast-paced environment in many institutions, there has too often been little attention paid to keeping stakeholders informed about the outcomes. However, institutions are encouraged to take the time to generate short-term wins and broadly disseminate the information.

The equity work at many institutions interfaces and has many interrelationships with existing programs and services. At some institutions, integrating the equity work into the college's culture can be a long and challenging process. Indeed, some practitioners in the field tell us that they do not bother to celebrate accomplishments because it takes so long to finish a task that when a goal is finally accomplished it can feel somewhat anticlimactic. This situation is the very reason we encourage institutions to generate and celebrate short-term wins; institutions must fight the feeling of "it is too much trouble to celebrate." Failure to generate short-term wins and recognize the contributions of team members can result in individuals or team members feeling bogged down in an unwinnable battle, and morale may suffer. Every win counts, no matter how big or small, and should be celebrated.

One president at a medium-sized college in the South told us that he believed that short-term-win victory celebrations were unnecessary since the equity work was what the college needed to do in the first place. He said, "I do not see the point. Why call out equity wins? Why not celebrate everything? Moreover, if you do that, when does the *real* work get done?" While we listened to this leader's message, we view equity work as the real work of the institution. In today's environment, it is not difficult to fall into the mindset of thinking that equity work is just another demand on an already overloaded institution. Unfortunately, some educators do not view equity work as essential to the real work of an institution. However, equity is an important aspect of the mission of community colleges. The concept of equity must be embedded into all aspects of the community college's business. The reality is that recognition of people's contributions to the equity agenda can be a good motivator for keeping them engaged in the work. Generating short-term wins can become an essential part of the institution's culture.

We have witnessed how recognition of a job well done after a team has completed a significant task can keep people going. Regardless of one's perspective about celebrating short-term wins, the truth is that most people need positive reinforcement and recognition. It is not enough to fall back on the age-old defense of "they get paid, so they should just do their jobs!"

While we can cite anecdotal examples of some ways that individual leaders generate and celebrate short-term wins, in far too many cases these leaders have not demonstrated meaningful ways of integrating victory celebrations into their ongoing leadership practices. Too often, they have neither implemented consistent individual employee recognition activities (beyond recognition of retirements or years of service awards) nor identified ways to recognize individuals or groups for the work taking place at the institution. Moreover, too often some leaders have shown by their inadequate attention to establishing measurable outcomes for equity initiatives that they have no data for which to generate short- or long-term wins.

However, the shortage of data was not the case at one college that we worked with in the Midwest region. This institution realized that generation of short-term wins for their equity work was an opportunity to reinforce the tenets of the college's strategic plan, culture, and core values. The college's employees also liked to play games and had established a culture of having fun at team meetings and other college gatherings. As a result, some of their meetings tended to revolve around games. That is why the Institutional Research Office staff felt comfortable developing a trivia game based on the accomplishments of the various committees working on the college's equity initiatives. While it may be easy to downplay the prospect of employees sitting around playing games, the reality is that a trivia game about the accomplishments of the project team assigned to examine barriers to student success went a long way (at this college) in developing a consensus around what the college needed to do to remove inequities from policies and practices around the equity agenda. The attention that emerged from playing the game also brought joy to the members of the committee; they appreciated the recognition that peers and the broader college community paid to their work.

It is difficult to summarize what institutions can do to celebrate short-term wins because each institution has its own unique culture and will have different milestones to celebrate. However, we do know that generating and promoting short-term wins must be a continuous process. Fundamentally, integrating equity into the culture, goals, and core values of the institution begins with employees; they are responsible for the progress of the college's equity efforts. Full recognition and generation of short-term wins can facilitate that progress. Generating short-term wins can also encourage employees who are not engaged in the institution's equity efforts to become involved in the transformation efforts at the institution.

8

CONSOLIDATE GAINS UTILIZING INSTITUTIONAL LEADERSHIP

Chapter highlights: In this chapter, the authors provide strategies for maintaining momentum while striking the balance of continuous change.

Leadership focus areas: Institutional infrastructure, institutional leadership, advocacy and mobilizing others, communication, and collaboration.

When an institution transitions into the stabilization of the equity agenda, many of the leadership competencies become increasingly important. In our experience, this phase of the implementation is where everyone's leadership is tested.

Once an organization has communicated short-term equity wins, the challenge of maintaining the momentum begins; the momentum must be sustained while change continues to occur. As previously mentioned, an equity transformation is a long journey. Leaders must be cautious in communicating the short-term wins along the way to ensure the bar is not set too high after the first win. The second and, perhaps, third win must create the same excitement and momentum. The strategies for sustaining the acceleration needed to become equity-centered institutions are multifaceted. In the end, it will take leadership from the EOT and CEO to embed equity into the culture of the college.

Remain Consistent

The EOT and CEO always have to be on the lookout for resisters to the transformational change process. The moment the detractors sense that the pressure is no longer on the pedal, they will emerge. The EOT and CEO have to be consistent not only in their messaging, whether it's short-term wins or implementation, but must also be consistent in their advocacy, transparency, and example in all actions related to equity. Kotter (2014) stated, "Whenever you let up before the job is done, critical momentum can be lost, and regression may follow" (p. 121). We have seen this at work and would take it a step further: *The job is never done, and it is imperative that not only the EOT remain consistent, but all leadership as well.*

Small interactions between leaders and faculty or staff can cause major setbacks in maintaining momentum in building a culture of equity. One college in the Midwest developed a leadership development institute for its senior and midlevel leaders that was anchored in the AACC's (2018) competencies for community college leaders. Anicich and Hirsh (2017a) suggested that middle managers must constantly oscillate between situations in which they have either low or high power. To encourage midlevel managers, senior leaders used monthly interactions between midlevel leaders and the senior leadership team, placing an emphasis on communication, presentations, and email communication.

This Midwest college used scripts with key equity-oriented phrases to provide consistent messaging for the midlevel team members. But there is always the chance for misunderstandings. For example, one president in the Midwest was publicly criticized for using the phrase "poor students." Actually, the word *poor*, in this context, was being used to create a sense of pity for the students; however, the comment was splashed all over Twitter to suggest that the president was opining that students were of a low economic class. The use of words in a culture of equity is one example of how a lack of consistency can create chaos and set the equity agenda back as if months of hard work never happened.

Recognize and Manage the Capacity for Change

Creating an equity-centered culture is a heavy lift in most institutions. In the college's equity transformation, what are the anticipated outcomes? At this phase in the transformation, leaders must ask themselves, if they have accomplished the outcomes, how the institution remains consistent and if that means they continue to change. Creating an equity-centered environment is a long road, and we have learned that every institution has a capacity for change. We are not suggesting that leaders stop moving, but the pace at this point should change.

Think about equity transformation like weight loss. Many models for weight loss suggest that one has to make a lifestyle change. We are taking the equity conversation in the same direction by suggesting that institutions make lifestyle changes. From a nutritional perspective, when a person enters into a lifestyle change, they may remove sugar and carbohydrates from their diet. They may add exercise to their daily activities. In the beginning, the weight loss may be huge, such as three pounds per week. However, at some point, the weight loss slows down. The body hits a plateau. . When a person has reached the plateau stage, it does not mean that the person reverts back to bad eating habits. The lifestyle change must be maintained, or the weight and related health issues will return. Lifestyle changes for the institution are no different than lifestyle changes for individuals.

Similar to the body in terms of weight loss, organizations have a capacity for transformational change. The CEO must recognize when the plateau occurs. Operational signs of the plateau in an organization may include the following:

- Operational systems that address equity for students and employees
- Procedures and best practices that close equity achievement gaps for students
- Procedures and best practices that reduce equity barriers in hiring employees
- Organizational structures that position the college to implement all operational procedures
- Systems that increase access for all
- Morale that improves dramatically and is measured (notice we don't say morale is high—we want to be realistic)

These are all useful signs that the institution can look for when moving the equity agenda forward. Another barometer for understanding when the institution has reached its capacity for change can be seen in the behavior of the people:

- People may begin to express frustration with constant change
- People may begin to create situations to stall change
- People may create interdependence between units, making change harder to accomplish (e.g., faculty and staff leadership teams may join together for a cause)

We have a great illustration of this scenario. At Dr. Beatty's institution, early in her tenure, she began to rapidly change the organizational structure to position the college to create a systemic approach to operations. The institution was realigned in such a way that some positions were eliminated, others were created, and others were changed. When the chief academic officer decided to take another position, Dr. Beatty saw an opportunity to align the executive-level leadership around a comprehensive student success model with a provost position—a position that would oversee academic affairs and student success/engagement.

While this is a popular trend in community college organizational structures and one that creates an opportunity to strategically align the institution around student success, many groups, especially the faculty, said, "That's it! No more changes." The faculty were not prepared to tolerate additional changes. From the faculty perspective, the organization had reached its capacity for experiencing change. Beatty took their concerns under consideration and recognized that even though the realignment was strategically sound, implementing the change was not in the best interest of the institution at the time. She moved forward with hiring a chief academic officer (CAO). Moving forward with the change to the provost model would have created revolt and chaos, disrupting all of the hard work that already occurred.

While this illustration is not focused on equity, it exemplifies that every organization has its capacity or "lid" for change (Maxwell, 2014). A good leader uses sound institutional leadership to recognize when dramatic change must become subtle change, but change nonetheless. In the CAO example, the right candidate was selected, a candidate who was focused on and understood the need for a comprehensive student success model.

The equity focus must continue as well. When the institution reaches its capacity, small, subtle changes can still occur. For example, once the big changes have occurred, the operational implementation of equity principles will continue to occur, just at a slower pace and probably less visible. It is important for the CEO to monitor and manage the change process as it unfolds. For example, regarding institutional culture, the CEO should be able to see that equity is anchored in practices and procedures. If not, the CEO will need to determine what factors need to be considered. Again, managing the equity vision means that there is constant change, but understanding the culture of the organization can be an indicator as to how fast the change occurs.

The CEO must also consider whether equity is embedded into the institutional infrastructure. In other words, the equity vision must be anchored into the fabric of the institution such as the budget and strategic plan. These are areas of change that will sustain the equity effort yet can be implemented at a slower pace since these are elements that are typically reviewed annually. Pace becomes important as the change continues to be sustained.

Work Smarter, Not Harder

It is very easy to suffer from burn out when striving to become an equity-centered institution. The push and pull in the relationship can become exhausting for the CEO and leadership team. The leadership competencies become extremely important in this phase. The primary components for continuing change rely on people and systems. Instead of playing checkers, now the leadership and equity operations team (EOT) must play chess. The chess game rests in institutional leadership fundraising/relationship cultivation, advocacy/mobilizing others, performance management, and student success. All these competencies should be used to develop the policies that will maintain momentum but, more importantly, engrain equity into the fabric of the institution.

When considering fundraising and relationship cultivation, there is both internal and external cultivation that takes the equity work to the next level. Internally, the EOT should implement a plan that continues to engage key stakeholders. As mentioned in chapter 7, people may continue to see this work as a fad; the interest has to be maintained. However, in this phase, the organization may consider hosting an information forum once a semester, coupled with an "equity institute" each summer. The semester meetings can serve as an opportunity for the champions to update the EOT on short-term wins. The equity institute, on the other hand, should be the annual opportunity to "reset" the equity transformation. In essence, in a retreat format, the EOT should ask the following:

1. What is working?
2. What isn't working?
3. What have we learned?
4. Where can we improve?
5. What are our next steps?
6. What data is available to support the direction that we need to take?

These six questions will serve to reignite the equity conversation and allow the EOT members to continue to cultivate their relationship with one another as well as develop relationships with internal stakeholders.

The external relationships should focus on developing partnerships for sustaining the equity work moving forward. The CEO will typically be the person responsible for leading these interactions. The CEO must assess, in collaboration with the EOT, whether the organization values equity and may want to make an investment that builds on the work completed thus far.

For example, a college focused on student equity and closing achievement gaps can consider the following:

- A long-term investment in scholarships targeting certain student groups
- A capital contribution to a success center for students
- A long-term investment in a mentoring program targeting specific populations (e.g., men of color, first-generation students)

These are just a few ideas where we have seen success and typically have had some shared interest between the college and regional foundations.

In addition to fundraising and relationship cultivation, governance, policy, and legislation become important when considering both the people and the systems. In this phase, accountability through governance, policy, and legislative work should be inserted to sustain an equity agenda at the college and at the local and state levels.

Use the governance structure to develop policies regarding performance management linked to the advancement of the equity agenda. First, work with and through the governance structure to develop a policy (if one doesn't exist) regarding the evaluation process. The purpose of using the governance structure is the need for continued buy-in from stakeholders in the advancement of the equity agenda process. If the leadership of the college creates a policy in isolation from other stakeholder groups, the policy may be perceived by faculty and staff as a top-down policy that is being imposed on other stakeholders. However, if the conversation begins with the EOT asking stakeholders to respond to the following question: How can we ensure that all employees are engaged and held accountable for deploying the strategies for a successful implementation of an equity agenda?," stakeholder groups are more likely to believe that they have a voice in way institution is addressing issues. We encourage institutions to create a situation where an idea emerges from the governance groups. Then, the EOT can identify faculty, staff, and administrators to partner with Human Resources or other administrative offices to develop equity-centered policies and procedures that align with the institution's overarching performance goals.

At most institutions, there is a system to develop performance goals. Through this system, a college could make it their practice to integrate an institutional goal system that includes equity on a continuous basis. In our experience, CEOs collaborate with the board of trustees to create goals for their boards and the institution. By modeling the way, the CEO should have a broad equity goal that is adopted by the board. The CEO equity goals should cascade down to the cabinet, and direct reports (division level), and then to other unit level employees throughout the institution. Using this cascading approach, policies and practices are enhanced to ensure that the equity agenda remains at the front and center of the evaluation process and overall institutional effectiveness.

The accountability does not stop at the college level. There is also equity work to be done at the state level. In some states, advocacy for a legislative agenda focused on equity becomes an imperative for higher education leaders. Some states need more growth in this area than others. For example, since the 1990s the California community college system has required each community college to develop and submit an equity plan. In Missouri, the conversations around equity are just beginning and only among the community college leaders in the state. We have seen the positive effects of the required equity plans in California. State-level accountability, especially when tied to funding, will likely yield action and results.

Recognize It's an Iterative Process

We view institutional transformations as an iterative process. Transformational changes such as equity are iterative insofar as they intentionally allow for "repeating" development activities and for potentially "revisiting" the same information with different stakeholders. Nearly all equity initiatives are incremental as well as iterative. For example, we suggested meeting with all stakeholders to communicate the equity vision to collect a variety of insights from those sessions to build the "real thing."

An equity-focused transformation is no different, probably more so. As is the case with most transformations, the more change that occurs, the more the college learns. An equity transformation is like peeling back an onion— one layer is pulled back only to find another stronger layer. It's important to understand that small changes, especially regarding people and systems, will naturally continue to occur in the learning process.

The change and drive toward an equity-centered institution will never stop. There are many reasons for constant change. First, community colleges are extremely nimble, and the population and issues are equally nimble. While the nimbleness is a great characteristic in some cases, when it comes to equity it can be problematic. For example, policies and procedures that were not needed 10 years ago are now necessary. As the population and needs of our students change, we will need to change our policies and procedures. The systems colleges use to provide data analytics on progress are always changing and require upgrades; as the systems change, business processes and training must change as well. In this process, according to Kotter (2014), it is difficult to have a complete sense of all the changes at the beginning of the change process. Institutional leadership is required to see an equity transformation through.

In addition, the level of change associated with the implementation of an equity agenda requires some level of focus. Therefore, the college may restart the phases outlined in this book on a smaller or larger scale depending on the (sub)issues that can emerge in the peeling-back-the-onion phase. Once the EOT determines its focus, additional foci can be considered after the primary efforts have demonstrated small wins. This strategy is supported in the book *The 4 Disciplines of Execution: Achieving Your Wildly Important Goals* by Chris McChesney, Sean Covey, and Jim Huling (2012).

The authors suggested that no organization can focus on everything at once; there must be focus for a successful implementation, even if that means going through the same process again with a different focus. Moreover, the authors posited that when it comes to attaining wildly important organizational goals, the role of the manager in the business execution process is critical. It is time for community college leaders to take another look at new and different ways to implement change. The role of educators is changing at all levels of the institution; it's time for leaders to understand that equity is the norm and not the exception. And it's time for community college leaders to tout how equity is imbedded in transformational change in higher education.

Establish Outcomes

At the beginning of this chapter, we provided some broad indications of success after an equity transformation. These successes will lead to four dominant outcomes for a college in this phase: more change, not less; more support from the people; and leadership from senior management and from below the senior ranks.

Change is an iterative process, which means that change is constant. The key to success with an equity transformation is managing continuous change. Consider a spider web as a metaphor. The center of the web is the equity vision; however, the center of the web cannot stand alone. To make a complete web that is useful to the spider, the web has to be developed and connected to a solid frame. The concept applies to the equity vision. In order for the vision to come to fruition, there are many people, systems, and processes that surround the vision that must continue to change until they can be anchored to the initial frame (the big changes). If each circle of the web is an indication of a cycle of change, it's easy to imagine the time involved in becoming an equity-centered institution. In fact, as the equity vision web is being spun, language will become very important. Perhaps *change* is not the word used; leaders can consider words such as *alignment, realignment, transformation*, or *transition*. Careful and strategic use of the communication leadership competency will be important to navigate the web of constant change to completely implement the equity vision.

In addition to the continuous change, more people will become involved to help bring the equity vision into reality and manage future change. In the initial phases of developing and implementing the equity vision, the EOT drives the process. Through phases 2 through 4 of the change process, many people across the institution will be engaged in implementing the equity vision. This broad engagement will naturally attract new pioneers into the fold. In any culture, there are those who want, actually crave, change, but initially they are skeptical of the possibility of change coming. This explains why communicating short-term wins in step 6 of Kotter's change model is so important. The more the college community can see progress with the equity vision, the more they are likely to want to become equity-centered institutions. The opportunity at this point is to create a broader EOT in a less formal way to implement and manage additional change. Unconsciously, the equity-centered change is making its way back to phase 1 and starting to spin another piece of the web.

The opposite may be true as well. Just as there will be those who crave change and alignment with the equity vision, there may be those who do not, and that's okay! There will be some natural attrition at the institution, especially when equity becomes the focus for moving the institution forward. It is likely that some people will confuse equity and equality, making the issue about race rather than the equitable resources and support infrastructure needed to have a quality employee and student experience. Also, given the new procedures to support the equity vision that will become part of the web, some will resist those changes as well.

There may be some stakeholders who the leadership team will have to coach into understanding the direction the college is going or into finding a better match for their employee experience. Once the equity vision is set, any opposition or intentional sabotage cannot be tolerated. Like potatoes in a bag, one rotten potato will make the entire bag rotten if the one rotten potato is not removed. The same is true in organizations. We do not make this analogy in a callous, insensitive way; we understand that a person's career can be affected when leading a change initiative. However, there are two aspects to consider: leadership and followship. There are many layers of leadership and followship. The latter is usually the most difficult aspect when implementing any change. Through the process of implementing an equity vision, those who choose not to follow will emerge and rot if not addressed immediately.

To continue the potato metaphor, we all have experiences where the smell of the rotten potato causes one to pull the potato out of the bag and cut off the rotten portion before the entire bag of potatoes goes bad to salvage some of the newly rotten potato. We have experiences where the same approach can happen when managing people. Good leaders can "smell" when a person is beginning to rot based on the employee's attitude and actions. Often, a courageous conversation can create a common understanding and remove the rotten portion. In these situations, active listening becomes important, because normally the leader can identify a role for the individual in implementing the equity vision. We have experiences where the somewhat "rotten" person can become one of the biggest supporters of the equity vision.

The last two outcomes that can be expected in this phase of the equity transformation are emerging leadership from the senior leadership team and from below. Everyone's leadership competencies will be tested, and the CEO may be surprised by the leaders who emerge in the process. Senior leadership may rise to the occasion as they maintain the level of urgency needed to maintain a focus on equity (Kotter, 2014). The senior leadership team is encouraged to keep equity at the "top of mind" as the college moves through the transformation process. There are simple strategies that can be used to ensure appropriate execution of the equity vision (McChesney et al., 2012):

- Establish the focused aspect of equity for the team to implement: Equity is a big subject that, at the senior leadership level and through the visioning exercises highlighted in phases 3 and 4, has been broken into many parts. The senior leaders should identify one aspect of the equity vision as a focus. In student services, for example, the focus may be on the student experience in advising.
- Include equity as a standing topic on weekly agendas: Whether there is a weekly team meeting or not, create a dedicated 15–30-minute timeframe where the senior leader and the team can discuss the approach and progress on equity.
- Create a competition around the focused aspect of equity: People, whether they recognize it or not, are competitive by nature. A competition will generate excitement for the equity vision. If, for example, the student experience in advising is the focus, and the vice chancellor (the senior leader in this case) in a multi-campus district has a team of Student Service Department deans responsible for advising departments on campus, the vice chancellor can create a competition around which the campus demonstrates evidence of providing an equitable advising session for students that leads to the student's subsequent enrollment. (If this competition were to continue, later the competition can add their subsequent success in courses.)

- Develop a scorecard for an equity competition: Most people like to have a visual image of progress. The scorecard supports the "cadence of accountability" necessary to lead an equity vision. The scorecard can be jointly developed with some individual flare. Continuing with the advising example, the vice chancellor can lead the team through the process of identifying metrics to build an electronic master version of the scorecard. People can individualize the scorecard by creating fun team names related to the vision, such as "Team Equity for All Students" or "Team Equity First." An additional opportunity to engage the group is to allow them to individualize their sub-team's scorecard for the campus.
- Share the results of the equity competition: The accountability continues by reporting the results in the weekly meetings. In this process, a reward system could be integrated as well.

Using the framework from *The 4 Disciplines of Execution* (McChesney et al., 2012) is an ideal strategy for senior leaders to maintain momentum and demonstrate leadership. This framework and other work happening at the college may inspire leadership from the lower levels of the organization to aspire to be accountable in implanting the equity agenda. The cadence of accountability will cascade through the organization. People who may not have cared in the past about the operations will now say to themselves, "If I have to care about equity and perform certain tasks for which I am being held accountable, I am no longer going to tolerate the passive attitude from you!" At the lower levels, people will begin to have their own conversations with those who are not on board with the equity vision or share their concerns with upper-level management.

To consolidate gains toward becoming an equity-centered institution, the leadership competencies will be tested. The senior leadership and management must remain consistent and recognize the institution's capacity for change. It's important to manage the equity transformation in a way that is nimble and flexible. Recognize that the planned approach may not be the only approach to overcome equity challenges.

9

ANCHOR EQUITY INTO THE CULTURE THROUGH GOVERNANCE AND REVAMPING THE INSTITUTIONAL INFRASTRUCTURE

Chapter highlights: This chapter discusses how the institution's culture has a major impact on whether the institution accomplishes the goal of becoming equity centered. It establishes the concept that anchoring equity into the institution's culture is like climbing a steep hill; the end result will likely create a positive learning environment for students and employees.

Leadership focus areas: Organizational culture; governance, institutional policy, and legislation; institutional leadership; institutional infrastructure; advocacy and mobilizing others; communication; and collaboration.

A t the beginning of this book, we focused on institutional culture. The second chapter and first phase of the transformation process was titled, "Create a Sense of Urgency for Equity Through the Existing Organizational Culture." The keyword is *existing* culture. If the equity transformation is done correctly, gradually there should be an impact on the institutional culture. Now, in this final phase of the equity transformation, it is important to be intentional and strategic about cultural change. Without a change in the culture, the equity transformation will not become rooted in the core fabric of the institution. As Kotter (2014) says, "Cultural change comes last, not first" (p. 153). Recognizing this, the last phase of the equity transformation is probably the hardest and most time-consuming—anchoring the equity vision into the culture of the institution.

The Challenge

The popular saying, "If it were easy, everyone would do it" rings true when transforming a culture to align with the equity vision. The challenge emerges as new equity-centered practices and policies regarding the people, structure, and systems emerge that are not aligned with the existing culture. Hence, the leadership and EOT must utilize the governance process and institutional leadership to penetrate the culture.

> *Culture* refers to norms of behavior and shared values among a group of people. *Norms of behavior* are common or pervasive ways of acting that are found in a group and that persist because group members tend to behave in ways that teach these practices to new members, rewarding those who fit in and sanctioning those who do not. *Shared values* are important concerns and goals shared by most of the people in a group that tend to shape group behavior and that often persist over time even when group membership changes. (Kotter, 2014, p. 148)

These two components of culture—norms of behavior and shared values—are difficult to change because sometimes they are not visible behaviors. For example, if an organization has a shared value to not trust the administration, then the behaviors of the members will exhibit the lack of trust. "Trust" is not a visible entity; however, the behaviors are sometimes very visible. Let's draw another example related to developing an equity-centered institution.

In chapter 1 we talked about the difference between equity and equality. We have also, throughout this text, discussed how conversations about equity often become courageous conversations because people automatically equate equity with a discussion about race. Leaders and individual contributors alike undoubtedly find themselves in situations where they need to be candid and carry out constructive conversations with others. When discussing the relationship between equity and its presence (or not) in an institution's culture, it is possible that the culture (or lack thereof) of equity is formed on the grounds of race or equality. Therefore, it is likely that the shared value is that all students are treated the same, and then the behaviors exhibited by personnel will likely be the same. In many cases, the shared values related to equity are established based on the college's long-term experience in dealing with equity issues. Likely, these shared values are created out of a sense of "they don't know what they don't know." This is where institutional leadership and advocacy become important to implanting an equity vision that is rooted in the culture over time.

As highlighted in chapter 4, most institutions have a governance structure anchored in the culture. This structure begins with the board down to the lowest level of the institution. In some colleges the governance process is strong, especially when there are bargaining units involved. While bargaining units and shared governance are two distinctly different things, they often influence one another and impact the desired change. The governance structure is the best place to begin to "take the temperature" of the institution to determine the gap between the existing behavioral norms and shared values and the equity vision.

Here's the approach: Every good leader should assess the effectiveness of a new implementation. Using the existing governance structure (board, faculty, and staff governance associations), strong communication skills, advocacy, and institutional leadership competencies, create conversations that can be called an "equity reset." These reset conversations should be under the guise of having implemented new components (people, structure, and processes) to support the equity vision. By hosting collaborative, open conversations about the equity vision and its implementation, the leadership can identify gaps.

For the equity reset conversation, the facilitator may want to launch a conversation in advance by providing context and thought-provoking questions via email. Consider grouping the questions based on the categories previously discussed, as these are the areas of the college that have the greatest opportunity to embed the equity vision into the culture:

People

1. Has the professional development training provided a new perspective about equity?
2. What evidence (if any) of behaviors have you seen that support the equity vision?

Structure

1. Does the institutional structure enhance or detract from the implementation of the equity vision?
2. How can we ensure the structure further complements the equity vision?

Systems

1. Is there adequate technological system support for the implementation of the equity vision on the ground?
2. Are there adequate policies and procedures to support the expectations of the equity vision?

By sending these questions in advance, participants will have time to think about detailed responses. Unlike the approach in chapter 2, the EOT could bring all governance structures together in one setting for this conversation. In fact, the authors have experience where a board member serves as the liaison with the equity committee and participates in discussions.

At the actual equity session, consider separating the attendees into groups, mixing the governance leadership. In other words, it's beneficial to have staff, faculty, and administrators mixed within each group, with at least one member of the EOT at each table. Allow them the time to share their prepared responses with one another in an effort to create one set of responses per table. At this point, facilitators should listen closely, noting the gaps in behavior that align with the equity vision. To take this exercise a step further, the facilitator can consider using the ideas presented to begin a discussion of shared values. There will likely need to be a part 2 and possibly part 3 to this conversation, but it will move the organization toward a list of shared values that, over time, will change behavior.

The Power of Culture

Have you ever seen an old tree? They can be recognizable because they have big roots. Sometimes, the roots are so big and deep they can do damage to pipes in a home. The same is true for culture. Without deep roots, when the CEO changes the behaviors may regress to the old culture.

To anchor an equity vision in the culture of the institution, the equity vision and cultural norms of the institution must be aligned. The collaborative conversations highlighted in the previous section will be valuable in this process. Through continued communication and collaboration, the core values that are aligned with the equity vision will become behavioral norms (this is the manifestation of the culture shifting) through the behavior of the hundreds of people in the organization. Consider a more simplistic example. Everyone has a routine at the start of the day. The routine may be a specific route to work. Every day, the same road is traveled. Soon, the route is taken with very little effort on the driver's part. People call this driving on autopilot. It's not autopilot; it's a behavior that "happens without much conscious intent" (Kotter, 2014, p. 159). When behaviors happen naturally and become a habit, that's when the culture will change.

In chapter 8 we addressed incorporating equity into the strategic plan and its policies. These approaches may also change the culture over time. The results of the policy development and implementation of the strategic plan are very important to the change process. When people see the results, the culture will begin to shift, especially if the results are better than the existing culture (Kotter, 2014).

Culture brings this process full circle. In chapter 1 we urged the reader to create a sense of urgency through the existing culture. Through this process, the culture should change, but that may not happen until long after the transformation has taken place. Leaders of the equity agenda have to be ready for the long haul. The culture of an institution takes a long time to penetrate, but, with strong collaborative leadership skills, it can be accomplished.

IO

PROMOTE EQUITY
IN THE FIELD

Chapter highlights: This chapter discusses equity from a national perspective and at three different institutional types. Karen Stout, president/CEO, discusses how Achieving the Dream (ATD), a national community college reform work, has led the way for many community colleges to engage in reform efforts through an equity lens. She shares the equity efforts of several ATD community colleges. Jorge Zeballos, chief equity and inclusion officer at Kellogg community colleges describes how a single community college defined equity and launched strategic efforts to embed equity in the culture of the institution. One of the authors, Kimberly Beatty, explains how a one college multi-campus system is focusing on equity in a region that is just starting to conduct equity-centered conversations. Ross Ryan, associate vice chancellor for student affairs, equity, and inclusion at the Colorado Community College Systems (CCCS) describes how the system's chancellor and governing board has lead the way for the 16 campuses to launch equity efforts stemming from the system's strategic planning efforts.

Leadership focus areas: Organizational culture, governance, institutional policy and legislation, institutional leadership; institutional infrastructure, advocacy and mobilizing others, communication, and collaboration.

As community colleges continue to roll out student success and completion initiatives, implementers face overcoming real-world obstacles. Whether it is developmental education issues or skepticism from constituent groups, the practitioners delivering programs and services to students are gaining invaluable information about how to address practical teaching and learning problems to successfully deliver services to students who need them the most. This chapter highlights activity in the field by placing the spotlight on the work of a national higher education nonprofit organization and several community colleges. This chapter will help sharpen insights about equity and provide useful resources. We have spent many hours visiting with and talking with practitioners about their equity work. Now, we want to give you the opportunity to do the same. In this chapter, we share equity in the field from multiple perspectives:

- Achieving the Dream—the national, nonprofit leader in championing evidence-based institutional improvement
- Kellogg Community College—A single community college system
- Metropolitan Community College—A multi-college community college district
- CCCS—A statewide community college system

These perspectives bring together a range of experts to present research, data, and equity-empowering strategies. This chapter of the book showcases national and local efforts that are redefining equity nationwide, offers insightful commentaries and critical analyses, and highlights leaders and policies that assert equity.

National Perspective

Higher education institutions must examine how their programs, policies and practices bridge economic and social inequities for their students. This examination will help institutions determine who has and has not benefitted from the services provided by the institution. In this section of the book, Karen Stout, president of ATD, discusses how some institutions in the ATD Network are leveraging resources to drive transformational change.

ATD: Background and College Transformation Model
by Karen Stout, President and CEO

For the past 15 years, ATD has been the leading college network championing evidence-based institutional improvement to help community colleges increase outcomes for low-income students and close opportunity gaps. The ATD network includes over 270 colleges in 44 states and the District of Columbia. ATD's award-winning colleges have been able to demonstrate double-digit degree completion gains and substantially close or eliminate opportunity gaps between subpopulations of students. All of this work is done in service of the nearly four million students who attend ATD colleges and universities to reach their life dreams of enhanced economic opportunities for their families (Achieving the Dream, n.d.a.).

Our college transformation model is based on a 3-year intensive capacity building effort designed to prepare colleges to implement large-scale change initiatives that will improve outcomes for students. The approach encourages campus-wide involvement at all levels to examine each institution's capacity in seven strategic areas: equity, teaching and learning, engagement and communication, strategy and planning, policies and practices, leadership and vision, and data and technology. Leadership and data coaches guide campus teams through an assessment of their strengths and opportunities for improvement followed by the building and implementing of an action plan based on identified priorities. Throughout the experience, teams use a variety of both quantitative and qualitative data and are benchmarked against peers through our partnership with the National Student Clearinghouse. Coaching and related supports come in the form of in-person visits and virtual coaching as well as issue-specific learning events like our Data and Analytics Summit and our larger full network convening known as DREAM, where colleges learn from leading national experts and their peers. Colleges who make progress on their fundamental capacities move into deeper more targeted work with us in areas such as holistic student supports, equity, and teaching and learning in order to further advance their transformation work over time.

Equity at the Forefront
Student access to and success in higher education continues to be impacted by the effects of structural racism and systemic poverty, and ATD focuses on both aspects in its work. Opportunity gaps among student groups reflect structural inequities that are often the result of historic and systemic social injustices. These inequities typically manifest themselves as the unintended or indirect consequences of unexamined institutional or social policies. The students who most suffer the consequences of the system of racism and economic privilege are our Black, Latinx, Asian Pacific Islander, and Native American students, as well as low-income and first-generation students. Teaching materials often signal to historically underserved students that they are less capable (e.g., criminal justice textbooks that only feature Black people behind bars), institutional practices such as placement tests and advisement that disproportionally guide minority students toward ineffective remedial courses, and larger national policies such as immigration legislation that inhibit certain students from receiving financial supports, continue to perpetuate these inequities.

Service providers who assist colleges must provide methods and safe spaces for administrators, faculty, staff, and students to address equity topics in depth. Surfacing institutional data is one route to uncover the system inequities, but then further steps must be taken to address the sources of these opportunity gaps tailored to the local context of the institution and surrounding community, create a vision for change that will eliminate gaps, and develop and execute a plan to make it happen. This is the core work of ATD.

ATD's institutional capacity framework is a comprehensive approach to addressing the emerging needs of the field to improve success results for all students, especially low-income students and students of color. The institutional capacity assessment tool (ICAT) is a self-assessment that helps colleges determine their current level of capacity in each of the seven key dimensions. Equity is one of the seven dimensions. We ask colleges to think critically about their commitment, capabilities, and experiences to equitably serve low-income students, students of color, and other at-risk student populations with respect to access, success, and campus climate. ATD is undergoing revision of the ICAT questions to more succinctly capture experiences, challenges, and breakthroughs that institutions are experiencing (Achieving the Dream, n.d.b.). Figure 10.1 highlights the scope of ATD's equity work.

Questions of equity disparities are embedded throughout our institutional capacity assessment tool and the resulting facilitated discussion that coaches lead in the first year of a college's experience with ATD. We require

Figure 10.1. ATD equity statement.

Community colleges are an indispensable asset in our nation's efforts to ensure and preserve access to higher education and success for all students, particularly students of color, low-income students, and other historically underrepresented student populations However, student access and success in higher education continue to be impacted by the effects of structural racism and systemic poverty. Achievement gaps among student groups reflect structural inequities that are often the result of historic and systemic social injustices. These inequities typically manifest themselves as the unintended or indirect consequences of unexamined institutional or social policies.

Achieving the Dream believes that access to a high-quality education in an inclusive environment is the right of all individuals and imperative for the continued advancement of a strong democracy and workforce. Achieving the Dream also believes higher education institutions have an obligation to work toward equity for their students. Equity is grounded in the principle of fairness. In higher education, equity refers to ensuring that each student receives what they need to be successful through the intentional design of the college experience.

Achieving the Dream expects colleges to dismantle the barriers facing underserved students. Colleges must routinely scrutinize structural barriers to equity and invest in equity-minded policies, practices, and behaviors that lead to success for all students (Achieving the Dream, n.d.c.).

colleges to consistently analyze their disaggregated data to find and manage toward the elimination of opportunity gaps, and coaches support campus leaders in directly discussing racial, sexual orientation and gender identity, and economic disparities as part of the college's journey toward transformation. Cross-functional campus change teams strategically address the systems, practices, and policy barriers that are contributing to the identified gaps.

ATD was among the first national higher education organizations to develop a public-facing equity statement and set of values to extend our stance on equity beyond our mission. ATD is continuously looking inward at its own equity practices and policies to model what we envision for our colleges.

Coaching Toward Equity
Community colleges are uniquely positioned to confront issues of racism, bias, and discrimination. Through a coaching model and community of practice, ATD colleges leverage expertise from others in the field solving challenging issues. This work is not easy, however, and is often abandoned because of the commitment required. ATD colleges are deeply committed because of the increasing demands of an evolving and diverse student population. ATD's equity statement challenges colleges to turn the magnifying glass inward and confront opportunity gaps and lack of attainment among students of color, women, and students in poverty. (See Figure 10.2.)

ATD coaches help colleges infuse equity in their work through crafting equity statements; developing and incorporating equity goals into college's strategic plans; facilitating courageous conversations on equity with a broad

Figure 10.2. Everett Community College equity snapshot.

Everett Community College (EvCC), joined the ATD network in 2010 and began working their leadership and data coaches to infuse equity more directly in their academic and other support activities. Spurred by the belief that "equity is non-negotiable and everyone's responsibility," in 2015 EvCC began a three-year, iterative process to explore holistically what equity means to their institution. Faculty, staff, students, K–12 partners, university partners and local employers engaged in the exploration process. The framework that emerged is the *5 Dimensions of Equity*™. Grounded in social justice, the five dimensions include equitable: aspiration, access, achievement, economic progress and engagement. The *5 Dimensions of Equity*™ are integrated into the work of teams across campus such as academic departments examining pass rates in gateway courses, individual faculty considering curriculum design and teaching methods, guided pathways subcommittees evaluating the effectiveness of advising processes and new student orientation, strategic enrollment management work groups, and student services offices who serve students with wide-ranging needs. In 2018, EvCC achieved the milestone of being awarded Achieving the Dream's Leader College of Distinction award for continued gains in student success rates that also narrowed opportunity gaps (Achieving the Dream, n.d.d.).

group of stakeholders; disaggregating data to identify opportunity gaps; dismantling structural barriers; and investing in equity-minded policies, practices, and behaviors using a structured and intentional process.

The process involves the following steps:

1. Learning about equity
2. Organizing for broad engagement
3. Starting with a focused set of data and relevant equity metrics, disaggregated by subpopulations
4. Building awareness of differences in performance
5. Deepening understanding of student experiences and motivations
6. Sharing data broadly
7. Using the data to develop evidence-based strategies and interventions

Equity for the Whole Student

Colleges working to deliver a holistic support experience demonstrate equity by ensuring that each student receives the personalized mix of support services they need to succeed in achieving their goals. (See Figure 10.3.) The approach involves collaborative, whole college teamwork to transform the student experience through the creation of an integrated comprehensive student support system (including advising, career planning, financial stability, and basic needs support) that enables students to develop and follow their chosen career, academic, and financial path while accessing the resources they need to be successful.

Colleges engaged in holistic student support work investigate and learn more about the students that the college serves while examining the students'

Figure 10.3. North Arkansas holistic support.

North Arkansas College (Northark) has been working since 2014 to design a more personalized, holistic support experience for their students, nearly 70% of whom have family incomes that qualify them for Pell grants. Early on in their work, Northark made sure to articulate the cultural issue of poverty as an institutional priority and thereby destigmatize students' need to access benefits and services. The college adopted the slogan "Northark Cares," reflecting an institutional commitment to meeting the daily needs of students over the long-term. Efforts to change the culture ranged from retraining faculty and staff for more personalized advising, to instituting mandatory success courses, to collecting and using better data to creating a food pantry and associated interventions to ensure students' financial struggles are surfaced and addressed. Underlying the work is a commitment to understanding each point of contact along the continuum of a student's experience as an opportunity to strengthen and personalize connections and to cultivate a sense of belonging in their students (Achieving the Dream, 2018b).

experience with the college's processes, policies, and practices. Colleges assess the structural, process, and behavioral barriers that hinder students from completing a credential. Central to holistic student support is to include the student's voice as part of the college's decision-making process in the redesign. Colleges must implement the structural, process, and behavioral changes to align college support services and workflows to meet identified student needs in a systematic and collaborative approach (Achieving the Dream, 2018a).

ATD's work is unique in the field in that it combines customized coaching support with deep content knowledge on the topic of academic and nonacademic student supports, including financial stability. It focuses on helping build institutional capacity to succeed with whole-college reform efforts through learning events and peer engagement and leveraging customized, on-the-ground coaching to help colleges successfully design and implement a holistic student support approach that provides more comprehensive, personalized, and proactive support throughout students' experiences (Achieving the Dream, 2019e).

Equity in Teaching and Learning
ATD developed the following four guiding principles that we believe can foster a culture of excellence in teaching and learning (Achieving the Dream, 2018b:

1. Full-time and adjunct faculty are using inclusive, evidence-based instructional practices to foster student learning. (See Figure 10.4.)

Figure 10.4. Columbus State Community College professional development series.

As part of its CRAFT (College Resources for Advanced Faculty Training) program, Columbus State Community College faculty engage in a series of professional development certificate sequences. One of these is focused on culturally responsive teaching and provides support in understanding key concepts such as macroaggressions, stereotype threat, and what it means to be an ally. As with its other certificate sequences on topics like cooperative learning, social psychological factors in learning, and student mental health, Columbus State makes clear that these professional learning experiences are grounded in evidence-based practice; have clear performance outcomes for faculty participants; and provide support for effective implementation. Furthermore, Columbus State has embedded this approach to faculty professional learning within a broader institutional structure by providing faculty professional learning opportunities that are well-designed, easy to access, and mandatory for faculty to be successful at the college (Achieving the Dream, n.d.b.).

2. Full-time and adjunct faculty are key collaborators in the college's student success efforts with staff and administrators in academic affairs and student affairs.
3. Students engage as active learners in an accessible, empowering, personalized, and supportive academic climate.
4. Institution embraces professional learning for continuous improvement and aligns these activities and related expectations in hiring, evaluation, and promotion.

As colleges realize each of these principles, they are creating the conditions to provide students what they need to be successful considering students' different lived experiences, strengths, and opportunities for growth. In our work to support colleges in building a culture of excellence in teaching and learning, we support the intentional design of learning experiences that mitigate the effects of structural racism and systemic poverty that plague traditional higher education curriculum and classrooms. This process requires an examination of academic materials, classroom processes, and instructional activities to identify, question, and remove bias and/or deficit-oriented practices that act as barriers to learning for underserved students, students of color, and low-income students. Colleges engaged in equity-minded teaching and learning practices commit to an investment in intensive professional learning that supports faculty and staff to develop the cultural awareness and competence needed to support culturally responsive practices. Each college's approach differs based on their campus context and the scope of implementation. Examples of effective equity-minded processes that inform faculty members' classroom practices in ways that support student success include the following:

1. Syllabi revision: Reorganize standard syllabi to incorporate welcoming and validating messaging and language that breaks down institutional and discipline-based jargon and expresses care for students' academic and nonacademic experiences (Center for Urban Education, 2018).
2. Culturally responsive curriculum assessment: Conduct a deep analysis of the curriculum content (texts, presentations, multimedia) to determine which voices are being privileged and which perspectives are misrepresented or absent (Bryan-Gooden et al., 2019).
3. Student participation–focused observation: Employ a peer observation tool that faculty use with each other to gain insight into participation patterns in their classrooms that can be analyzed by student demographics (Gray, 2019).

Hopeful Next Steps

As highlighted in the provided college examples, community colleges serve a diverse student population who come to class with enriched life experiences, backgrounds, and varied academic preparation. ATD's equity statement is a call to action for colleges to take responsibility for their part in a student's educational journey and to dismantle any barriers in the way of student success. Since ATD's network of colleges is vast and includes both rural and urban institutions, we recognize how they are meeting the call to close opportunity gaps among underserved populations and thinking creatively about ways to support students outside of the classroom. As a step further, ATD is positioning itself as a thought leader and change advocate for institutional equity reform among our network colleges.

ATD's network colleges are differentiating themselves as leaders in the higher education equity conversation by connecting missions to necessary student success metrics that show progress toward closing gaps. Colleges that are welcoming and diverse places free from inequities become the model for the communities they serve. Whole-college transformation occurs when the whole student is considered as a value add to the institution. Only through conversations around equity can this occur in lasting and meaningful ways for students' futures. We have a long road ahead, but our network of colleges is up for the challenge to positively impact every student.

Three Institutional Perspectives

This section provides an overview of how three different institutional types launched their equity efforts. The topic of equity is very complex and evolving, and institutions will move back and forth along a continuum of best practices. For this reason, we reached out to several community colleges to collect data about equity work taking place at their institution.

Kellogg Community College, Metropolitan Community College, and the CCCS were strategically invited to provide a snapshot of equity work taking place at their respective institutions: Kellogg is a single-college district, Metropolitan is a one-college multi-campus district, and the Denver Community College System is a statewide system.

Kellogg Community College: Jorge Zeballos, Chief Equity and Inclusion Officer

Kellogg Community College was founded in 1956 by the Battle Creek Board of Education. In 1970, voters created an area-wide college district supported by local tax dollars. KCC, which has sites in Battle Creek, Albion, Coldwat er, Hastings, and the Fort Custer Industrial Park, offers 59 pre-professional transfer curricula, 35 associate degree programs, 28 certificate programs, six categories of professional certifications, and a variety of short-term, non-credit courses. Kellogg Community College (KCC) serves approximately 8,400 students annually via five campuses, customized training, and online coursework. The college was fully reaccredited by the Higher Learning Commission of the North Central Association of Colleges and Schools most recently in 2012.

In 2014, the college received a 3-year grant of $2.1 million to establish the Center for Diversity and Innovation (CDI). The CDI's mission was to help organizations in the City of Battle Creek implement effective racial equity practices. Although CDI's work was mostly externally focused, its presence helped catalyze some internal movement related to equity and inclusion. CDI was able to use its funding to bring a speaker, Jamie Washington, in 2016, who facilitated a couple of sessions for staff, faculty, and administrators. CDI also offered a learning lab called White Men and Allies (WMAA) that explored issues of race, gender, and sexual orientation. An equity and inclusion committee with a new charter was created and began meeting in the summer of 2017. The vision of the new committee is to create an environment that promotes the advancement of equity through learning and understanding. Its mission is to regularly assess the systems, culture, and climate at the College through an equity lens and develop recommendations that foster a more inclusive culture for students and employees.

The Equity and Inclusion Committee (EIC) has been the main driver of the equity work at KCC. The EIC is composed of three members of the president's core team: chief HR officer, dean of institutional effectiveness and library services, and the executive director of the Center for Diversity and Innovation. There are four faculty members, two directors, an academic advisor, an account manager, a secretary, and a scholarship technician. In addition, the work is supported by the president, the vice president (VP) of instruction, the VP of student and community services, the executive director of KCC's foundation, the dean of enrollment services and financial aid, the dean of arts and sciences, the dean of students, and the chief communications officer. There are also several other staff and faculty members who are strong supporters of equity and inclusion, although they are not members of any of the formal structures KCC has in place to implement this work. The Equity and Inclusion Committee held a 2-day retreat as it was launched; the goal was to build a base of understanding related to the work of equity and inclusion and to build strong relationships among the members.

Based on his prior experience with equity and inclusion work and given that most employees had not received any equity training, the executive director of the CDI made a determination that what KCC needed to do first was to implement an equity capacity-building process for everyone at the college. The aim was to establish a common foundational understanding of what equity and inclusion mean, as well as build an understanding of what an institutional practice should look like at KCC. In addition, these sessions were designed to generate buy-in across the institution. The goals that were developed for the EIC were already embedded in the strategic plan that was developed in 2016, which included equity as one of its pillars. The EIC also determined that KCC needed to conduct a climate survey to establish a baseline for how different groups experience the college. The development of the survey started in the fall of 2018; it was implemented in the spring of 2019, with the results delivered in the summer of the same year. With the capacity-building process ending in the fall of 2019 and the climate survey results in hand, the next steps will be designed based on the findings of the survey as well as what has been learned through the capacity-building process.

Communication is an ongoing challenge in general at KCC. The EIC is working hard to implement an effective communication strategy, primarily to our internal community. A major challenge in implementing a strategy is the fact that we do not have a person or office dedicated to the work of equity and inclusion, so a task like this is hard to accomplish. Since the implementation of the equity capacity-building process, the conversations about equity have increased dramatically across the college. People feel more confident, have language and concepts, and have developed the comfort to speak on issues of equity.

There were no obstacles as we launched our equity initiative. Since the launching of the initiative and the implementation of the equity capacity-building process, we have encountered some resistance from some staff, although this is a very small number of people. The only structure we have in place at this point is the EIC, although it is important to point out again that many senior leaders also support the work and actively participate in the initiative. No new people have been hired for the equity work, which means that this work is an addition to the work responsibilities that every member already has. Our strategy with the few people who are resisting is to continue to engage and provide a rationale for the importance of equity work as an attempt to make sure that people feel their concerns are heard but also to be clear about why the college is committed to this work.

As a result of the steps we have taken, more staff are having conversations about equity more frequently. The hiring process is being revised to include more equity practices, such as implicit bias training for search committee members. Equity conversations are being included as part of the first-year seminar experience. An equity statement was approved by the board of trustees in 2018. We have not done any official celebration of these accomplishments. We certainly see significant movement based on what has been invested in this work. Equity-related questions were added to the CCSSE assessment conducted in 2019.

KCC has established a set of key indicators for faculty/staff and students that we will monitor on a yearly basis. The EIC and president's core team have developed a set of equity goals for the 2019–2020 academic year. In addition, specific goals have been created based on the results of the equity climate survey,

The college is in the process of establishing a chief equity and inclusion officer position to head the newly created Office of Equity and Inclusion. There is an institutional commitment to include equity-specific goals in the new strategic plan that will be created this academic year (2019–2020).

Metropolitan Community College: Kimberly Beatty, Chancellor

Metropolitan Community College is one college with five campuses. Metropolitan Community College (MCC) is the oldest and largest public institution of higher learning in Kansas City, Missouri, founded in 1915 as the Kansas City Polytechnic Institute. The Junior College of Kansas City, as it was known starting in 1919, was one of the first schools in the country to award an associate degree. Today, MCC offers 125 associate degree and certificate programs.

For the last 8 years, the institution did not have a true Office of Institutional Equity. Title 9 issues were becoming more frequent, and the lack of diversity in the faculty and facility ranks was disturbing. Not only internally, but externally, the college did not have a defined process to ensure that diverse suppliers were selected or had an equitable opportunity to compete for business. As a result, the Black and Hispanic community began to lose confidence in the ability to be able to become employed and/ or supported at the institution. To that end, there was no infrastructure to support equity.

With the arrival of the new CEO to the institution, there was a framework for a strategic plan, and diversity and equity were principles (values) built into the plan, yet there was no infrastructure to support it. There was a person who represented a "diversity" office; however, the office hosted events without any real connection to how the information applied to the attendees' daily work. Within the last year, the college hired an executive director of equity and inclusion. The executive director's first charge was to develop the tactics to support the strategic plan. Within the college's strategic plan, the unit goals cascade down from the CEO goals. It starts at the top. In most performance management systems, there are strategies or expectations associated with each goal. The employees are then evaluated based on whether they completed the strategies to complete the goal. When employees fail to accomplish goals, a plan for remediating the situation is developed. Over time, all employees will understand the commitment the college has to equity by embedding it into the performance management system.

Working through the existing governance structures, the executive director has a blank slate in developing an intentional approach to equity and inclusion at the college. Currently, MCC has diversity and inclusion councils on four of the five campuses. There is also a district-wide diversity and inclusion council with representation from the campus councils. The executive director will work with and through these councils to develop that strategic approach.

The first step, however, will be administering the equity assessment at the campus and district levels. Thus far, the college has only administered the assessment to the campus leadership team.

MCC is in the early phase in developing an equity vision statement that will be communicated broadly. The college has not yet taken any steps to implement the vision as we are just getting started. With a new executive director who is dedicated to this work, our biggest obstacle is the institutional culture and the culture of the Midwest. Everyone in this region and the institution is "kind" and really don't know what they don't know. It just simply has not been the focus of the institution because it is not the focus in this region. This perspective makes it very difficult to change, but it will happen over time.

CCCS: Ross Ryan, Associate Vice Chancellor for Student Affairs, Equity, and Inclusion

CCCS comprises the state's most extensive system of higher education. It serves as the primary provider of access and opportunity to higher education, especially for students of color and those from low-income families. Its 13 colleges deliver instruction in career and academic programs to more than 137,000 students annually, both online and at 40 distinct physical locations statewide. CCCS also oversees secondary and postsecondary career and technical education (CTE) programs across the state. Specifically, CCSS has CTE programming in 162 districts statewide. In middle schools, there are 144 programs in 129 schools in 55 districts. There are 1,411 high school programs in 183 schools located across 141 districts. The postsecondary level has 553 CTE programs across 19 community and technical colleges and within the Department of Corrections. Colorado's community colleges, the earliest of which opened its doors in 1925, have played a vital role throughout much of the state's history. The diverse programs offered by CCCS today are the product of a long tradition of providing accessible, affordable educational opportunities to students across the state who seek to improve their lives.

Chancellor Garcia, in his role for about 18 months, catalyzed launching the system-wide equity initiative in the CCCS. The equity journey was set from the system's strategic plan, the chancellor, and the state board. The strategic plan provided the platform for the system to create a new position focused on equity and inclusion (the first in CCCS history), as well as the equity campaign DIALED into Equity (Diversity, Inclusion, Achievement, Learning, Exploration of Data, and the Deconstruction of Equity). Deconstruction purports to show that language, especially ideal concepts such as equity, requires systematic examination to determine what is meant by the use of the term. CCCS used the term *deconstruction of equity* to demonstrate the act of breaking the Equity terminology down into its separate parts in order to understand its meaning and to arrive at a common definition of equity throughout the system. System-wide conversations entitled Deconstruction of Equity were held at each location in the system.

The system's equity work is supported and championed by the state board. Commenting on the action taken by the CCCS, Joe Garcia said, "We need to recognize that people are different and they bring different perspectives to our campuses. We need to welcome, learn about, and honor those perspectives."

CCCS launched the equity agenda for three primary reasons: There exist significant equity gaps in student outcomes; equity is aligned with the system's mission, and investment in erasing equity gaps ensures that the system is responsive to the communities served. The system is committed to using disaggregated data to identify equity gaps and to make informed decisions to support and document the work that is taking place.

The Equity and Inclusion Council was created to serve as an advisory board to system and college leadership and to be a thought leader in the areas of equity and inclusivity. The council, now led by the new associate vice chancellor for student affairs, equity, and inclusion, was created by the vice chancellor of academic and student affairs, Landon Pirius, after receiving authorization from Joe Garcia's predecessor in February of 2018. Pirius assembled the group using one direct appointment from each of CCCS's 13 college presidents and system office staff and invited community or equity experts as necessary. By June of 2018, the council had a mission, vision, and goals and began to meet with newly named Chancellor Joe Garcia. These meetings resulted in the recommendation and approval of the associate vice chancellor of student affairs, equity, and inclusion position. The council is role-modeling the work for the system colleges. It continues to focus on working collaboratively to support and set system-wide standards for inclusive excellence, closing the equity gap for students, diversifying the system and college workforce through inclusive hiring practices, and improving the retention of underrepresented employees (CCCS, 2020). While the council works well together, college presidents must ensure that each council representative has a voice on their respective campus and that each has a direct line to the college president.

To support the work of the Equity and Inclusion Council and the system commitment to equity, each president within the system has been charged with leading equity and inclusion efforts at their college and signing the "CEO Action Pledge for Diversity and Inclusion" (The Pledge). The Pledge centers on three main commitments: create a safe environment where people can understand the culture and everyone can evolve, implement and expand unconscious bias education, and be authentic and transparent on success and failures throughout the process. The three areas ensure that the culture and environment of institutions and organizations are environments where diversity, equity, and inclusion can be celebrated and learned from at all times.

In May 2019, Northeastern Junior College became the first college in the CCCS to take the CEO action pledge. The CCCS office and Northeastern Junior College, along with other organizations such as the City of Sterling, Sterling Regional Medical Center, and the Logan County Chamber of Commerce, pledged to support advancement in diversity and inclusion within the workplace by working collectively across organizations and sectors and by signing The Pledge.

Along with the public event to sign the pledge, the college hosted a "Deconstructing Equity" presentation by Dr. Ryan Ross, CCCS's associate vice chancellor for student affairs, equity, and inclusion, who leads the system's Equity and Inclusion Council. Ross said,

> One of the things we're excited about in our system is moving in a direction where all of our CEOs, our presidents, are signing onto the CEO Action Pledge. As a system, we decided to have our presidents' take on the pledge and look at how we do our work. From our perspective, one of the things that we do very well is there is a lot of initiatives that are already happening; we just haven't done an outstanding job of telling our story. (Jones, 2019)

Each college in the system was expected to complete an equity and inclusion plan by June of 2020. The future of the system's equity work centers on becoming a system of colleges where everyone thrives and where equity gaps do not exist. The key strategies to accomplish this overarching goal are as follows:

1. Leadership championing equity work in the system (all presidents are expected to sign The Pledge)
2. Professional development
3. Focusing on teaching excellence with an equity lens
4. Creating equity and inclusion councils at every institution
5. Providing resources to engage in the work
6. Creating spaces of grace (the term *spaces of grace* was used to describe spaces where individuals can shield themselves from uncomfortable or dissenting viewpoints) for their work to be inclusive and supportive of learning

The Equity Road Tour is the initial step the system used to communicate and demonstrate a system commitment to equity work. This tour was in addition to the System Equity and Inclusion Council meetings every other month on a different campus. The road tour consists of an address from the chancellor, and equity training session conducted by the associate vice chancellor for student affairs, equity, and inclusion and the college president, along with other CEOs from the immediate community signing the CEO pledge.

The primary obstacle faced by the system in launching and operationalizing the equity work has been and continues to be engaging all stakeholders in the equity effort at a meaningful level. Previous attempts on individual college campuses weren't always successful, and in some cases have made many reluctant to engage in meaningful equity conversation, let alone the work. One of our goals is to explain equity in terms that will enable everyone to know how it is used in the system. The end result will be a reintroduction of equity and inclusion in a way that involves everyone in a collegial manner and provides educational opportunities along the way while avoiding the "doom and gloom" judgmental approach that often shuts people down before the work is event started.

Some evolving strategies to promote the equity work will include external speakers whose messages align with CCCS goals and philosophy, creating equity awards within our student affairs and student leadership conferences, professional development for employees and presidents to empower them to support equity work at the campus level, and charging the Equity and Inclusion Council with advising system leadership on equity and inclusion perspectives.

CCCS continues to invest in the advancement of the equity work as evidenced by creating the associate vice chancellor for student affairs, equity, and inclusion's position, allowing time for council members to participate on the council, conducting system-wide equity tours, providing professional development opportunities for employees, and requesting that each president sign the CEO action pledge.

The equity work at the system office and on our campuses is ongoing. CCCS efforts will continue to focus on teaching excellence, creating councils at each school, professional development for employees, and using equity gap data to inform decision-making. College and system leadership will take steps to ensure that the work moves at a pace where no one is left behind. CCCS is working to better understand equity gaps with open and honest conversations and is taking steps to apply resources to close equity gaps. At the system level, the chancellor and the board have clearly communicated that, while the associate vice chancellor for student affairs, equity, and inclusion and the Equity and Inclusion Council may be leading the effort, *everyone* is expected to be engaged and responsible for equity and inclusion work.

II

FOCUS ON EQUITY
IN ACTION

Chapter focus: In this chapter, we present the results of the pilot study. We share our methodology and a summary of the collected data from three institutional types. This chapter provides an illustration of what an equity-centered institution looks like after going through the various stages of transformation.

Leadership focus areas: Practically all of AACC's leadership competencies are identified in this section—across the equity assessment continuum; evidence of leadership is reflected.

The authors are long-term practitioners in community colleges. We were inspired to write this book because it is not enough to just talk about equity; we sought to interact with leaders at different institutions to determine what is taking place with their equity work. We envisioned that input from other practitioners in the field would add additional insights about how equity work is not a "one-size-fits-all" proposition. In this book, we begin the conversation about transformational change through an equity lens with the hope that other practitioners might see how the use of a change model can enhance their efforts to promote equity-centered practices throughout the institution.

We do not plan to stop with this book. Our goal is to continue examining equity work in community colleges through our own work in the field, personal interviews with other practitioners, and surveys. We utilized a mixed method approach for collecting data for this section of the book, and the findings from our conversations and survey will be used to advance our long-term efforts. Through our contacts in the field, we employed a convenience sample of three different institutional types to querying leaders about the work taking place at their institutions.

To gain perspectives about institutional readiness for equity, we used the Institutional Equity Assessment that was discussed in chapter 2 (see Appendix A). The Institutional Assessment for Equity was adopted from the "Self-Assessment Rubric for the Institutionalization of Diversity, Equity, and Inclusion in Higher Education" (NERCHE, 2019). For purposes of this publication and recognizing that diversity, equity, and inclusion are three different principles, the authors modified the assessment to focus on equity. We collaborated with Dr. Melissa Giese to conduct a pilot study of equity efforts from three institutions. The remainder of this chapter focuses on the results from the pilot study.

The Methodology for the Survey

The primary purpose of the pilot study was to determine the institution's readiness to take a transformational equity challenge. The institutional equity assessment served as a tool for us to gather information about the college's ability to change and assess existing processes and resources available to support equity issues. The rubric proved useful in identifying gaps in the institution's structure, processes, and culture that may require radical transformation to ensure that equity is at the center of the decision-making at the institution.

The institutional assessment for equity is composed of six dimensions or sections. Each dimension includes components or statements to rate or characterize it. Additionally, there was an opportunity to provide evidence and comments regarding the rating for each dimension and its respective components. Institutional readiness scale scores were calculated for each institution type based on the total responses to the assessment items. The overall sum of responses across the entire assessment determined the level of institutional readiness for equity.

The institutional assessment for equity was converted into an online survey via Survey Monkey by the Metropolitan Community College's, Kansas City, Office of Institutional Research. A survey link was created and distributed to one college contact at each institution. The institution contacts then shared the survey with an executive leadership team member for completion. There were three institutions and 19 leaders asked to participate in the assessment. A total of 18 leaders (94.7%) completed the assessment between August 12, 2019 and September 1, 2019.

Section 1: Institutional Evaluation

The assessment data is presented in an aggregated format and then disaggregated by each dimension. There are six dimensions on the equity assessment:

four representing the institution, staff, students, and administrative leadership dimensions and two dimensions representing faculty:

- Dimension 1: Institution. This dimension measures the extent to which there is a shared definition of equity and how broadly it is understood throughout the institution. It also measures the degree to which constituents participate, the level of financial support toward equity, and the degree to which equity becomes integrated into the campus culture.
- Dimension 2: Faculty (engagement). This dimension measures the degree to which the faculty take ownership of equity and see it as essential to the academic core of the institution.
- Dimension 3: Faculty (teaching and learning). This dimension takes a look at practices and the degree to which faculty are involved in the implementation and advancement of pedagogy, research, scholarship and services related to equity
- Dimension 4: Staff. This dimension focuses on the level of staff engagement and involvement with regards to the implementation and advancement of equity.
- Dimension 5: Students. The student dimension measures the extent to which students have the opportunity to learn about equity, are aware of these opportunities, engage in these opportunities, and play a leadership role in the development of diversity on campus.
- Dimension 6: Administrative leadership. This dimension measures the extent that senior leadership demonstrates commitment and ensures the institution provides substantial resources, support, and accountability toward the equity effort.

In this section, noted differences between institution types are discussed to provide broad-based perspectives on the dimensions. The overall analysis of the quantitative data for each dimension showed that the institution and administrative leadership dimensions had the highest overall mean scores. The student dimension had the lowest overall mean score.

Specifically, the institution and administrative leadership dimensions contained the top four highest scoring assessment items. In general, the results showed that administrative leadership has knowledge and awareness of equity and supports the coordination of equity efforts. Eighty-eight percent of the respondents reported that their institution has professional development activities that include equity. The majority of respondents (83%) reported that initiatives or transformation efforts include equity at their institutions. (See Figure 11.1.)

Figure 11.1. Equity assessment dimension scores by institution type.

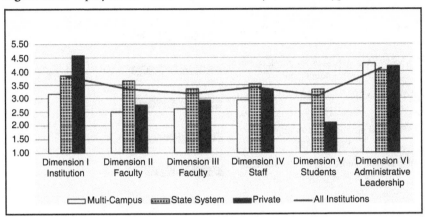

Respondents reported that opportunities for growth existed by providing incentives to staff and faculty for the development of equity engagement. Additionally, respondents expressed the need for more rewards for students and staff to be engaged in equity efforts. Specifically, increasing faculty engagement in research that incorporates equity was an area of focus for all institutional types. (See Figure 11.2.)

The results showed some variation between institution types and the dimension scores. The multi-campus institution had lower mean scores for all dimensions except students and administrative leadership as compared to the state system and private institutions. (See Figure 11.3.) The private institution had the lowest score for the student dimension, and the multi-campus

Figure 11.2. Equity assessment items with highest agreement.

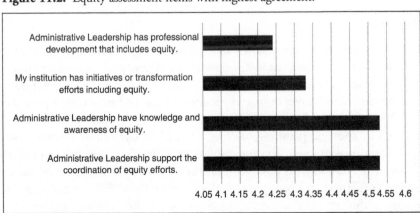

Figure 11.3. Equity assessment: Items with lowest agreement.

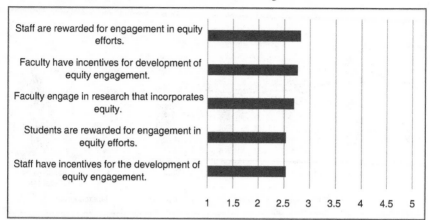

institution had the highest mean score for the administrative leadership dimension. Another notable difference was in the institution dimension. For this dimension, the private institution scored substantially higher than the multi-campus and state system institutions.

After each dimension, participants were asked to provide evidence (a narrative statement) to support their perspective or engagement. A qualitative analysis of the comments was conducted to provide common themes. Overall, a review of the comments shows that the majority of institutions are in the early stages of their equity work. Although the idea of equity work is not new to the institutions surveyed, the majority of comments showed that intentional efforts were recent and institutions are in the early stages of moving from conceptualization of equity to execution. The respondents reported that colleges are engaged in equity work It is too early to determine if this work will lead to transformation of practices at the colleges.

Dimension 1: Institution

Quantitative data for dimension 1 shows that 72% of leaders surveyed agreed or strongly agreed that their institution has a strategic plan focused on equity and 67% have a mission including equity, whereas 83% indicated that their institution has initiatives or ongoing student success efforts including equity.

The majority of evidence/commentary from respondents focused on four areas: strategic planning, staffing, council or committee involvement, and additional training and/or professional development opportunities. Some of the respondents observed that their institutions had recently added equity into their strategic plans and mentioned specific commitment to equity within the institution's mission, vision, and/or values. Additionally, many participants stated they had recently added a staffing position to focus efforts as well as developed councils and committees to further the equity work. Participants reported that different types of training or professional development were provided at their institutions such as training for intercultural competence, implicit bias and equity, leadership academies, equitable hiring, and cultural inclusion.

Dimension 2: Faculty (Engagement)

Most participants (71%) reported that faculty are knowledgeable and aware of equity; however, support of equity and demonstrating leadership efforts to advance equity are reportedly not as evident. The majority of participants shared evidence of activity, including faculty participation in equity efforts such as planning, inclusive pedagogy, professional development, and serving on committees, to promote equity efforts. One college offers stipends for curricular transformation and another offers release time for participation in equity committees.

Dimension 3: Faculty (Teaching and Learning)

Dimension 3 focused on faculty teaching and student learning. Again, the level of knowledge and awareness of equity in relation to faculty disciplines (53%) is higher than their responses to items focused on utilizing equity resources and incorporating equity into curriculum and teaching practices. Forty-one percent of executive leadership reported that their faculty use teaching and learning resources that incorporate equity. Thirty-five percent indicated that their faculty develop an equity-focused curriculum and student outcomes focused on equity, while only 29% indicated that faculty incorporate equity in teaching and learning.

In the comments section for this dimension, one participant noted that while their faculty have been knowledgeable about equity for some time, they have seen a real shift with faculty being "eager" to learn more. The institution has made equity a priority. Another respondent mentioned that some faculty have embedded equity into their teaching strategies. Some faculty have disaggregated student data to analyze equity gaps. Comments from participants showed that some of the institutions were not yet engaging faculty to the same degree as other employees.

Dimension 4: Staff

The percentage of executive leaders who indicated that staff have knowledge and awareness of equity was greater (88%) than was for faculty (71%). Staff were also rated higher on being involved and supportive of equity (88%). Seventy-six percent of executive leaders reported that staff demonstrate leadership efforts to advance equity.

The majority of comments documented the presence of staff engagement opportunities. Staff activities focused on equity were primarily around committee membership and professional development participation. There were few rewards or incentives mentioned for staff; however, one institution does have an annual Equity and Inclusion award available for staff and/or faculty.

Dimension 5: Students

Some of the lowest scores in this dimension fell within the student dimension, indicating that efforts to involve students have not yet been infused throughout the institutions surveyed. Less than half of executive leaders believed that students at their institutions were knowledgeable and aware of equity, involved and supportive of equity and/or demonstrated leadership efforts to advance equity.

The comments show that the participating institutions have not yet engaged students in equity efforts. There comments centered around two dynamics regarding students: direct student engagement and institutional evaluation of student success. Overall there were fewer examples provided as evidence to support student engagement in equity efforts. Student engagement was limited to experiences, including new student orientation, special programming, student leadership positions, and club participation. Many institutions discussed evaluating student success and had key performance indicators established. Only a couple of institutions are looking at equity gaps with institutional data.

Dimension 6: Administrative Leadership

Executive leaders indicated that 94% support the coordination of equity efforts but only 59% of administrative leadership develop a policy that includes equity. Two-thirds reported that their institution had a designated position to support and coordinate equity efforts, while 71% stated that funds were allocated to support equity.

Many members of the administrative leadership teams are engaged in equity efforts through committee or council membership. Evidence provided about the institutional leadership was focused around positions that existed specifically to lead the equity agenda. Although a couple of institutions had established positions, there was more mention of recent positions being created and some added as a part of the executive leadership. Additionally, there was specific mention of funding in the budget being tied to equity efforts.

Section 2: Institutional Readiness

This section focuses on the stages of institutional readiness. A score was calculated from participants' responses to each question. The possible scores ranged from 37–185, with the following categories defined as follows:

1. Emerging (37–73)
2. Developing (74–110)
3. Transforming (111–147)
4. Informing (148–185)

Assessment results indicate the level of readiness for equity overall and by institution type. The classification category based on scale scores is provided in Figure 11.4. The aggregate level of readiness for equity score on the assessment was 124 or transforming. There were minor differences in scores between institution types. Although all three institution types fell within the transforming classification, the highest scale score was reported by the state system followed by the single-campus institution. The large multi-campus institution received the lowest scale score. However, it is important to note that there was only a difference of 10 points between the top rating and lowest-rated institution type.

When data was disaggregated, there were more differences shown between the colleges within the state system. Although the state system's overall score as a system was transforming, four colleges within the system had higher scale scores, which classified their level of readiness as informing. One college in the state system had a score that fell within the developing

Figure 11.4. Level of institutional readiness.

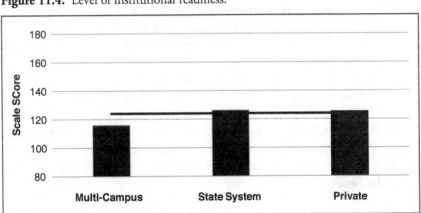

stage. This indicates that some of the colleges in the state system are further ahead in advancing their equity work.

Although this survey was a small sample size, given the diversity of the participating institutions, it provides insightful data about the equity work that is happening in the field. Essentially, there is still a lot of training and development at all levels of the institution to ensure that equity is at the center of how an institution moves forward.

Key Findings

An analysis of the findings revealed that institutions are practicing a wide range equity-centered activities to promote student success to include:

- Administrative leadership has knowledge and awareness of equity and supports the coordination of equity efforts.
- Institutions have professional development activities that focus on equity.
- Institutional type made a difference in the stage of equity readiness.
- The majority of institutions are in the early stages of their equity work.
- Most institutions have a strategic plan focused on equity, and most have a mission statement that includes equity.
- There is a need for more rewards for students and staff to be engaged in equity efforts.
- Institutions have not engaged students in the equity work.
- Institutions do not appear to be using their institution's data to explore equity gaps.
- Institutions have designated positions, councils, and committees to support and coordinate equity efforts.
- Institutions are allocating funds to support equity.
- Institutions are providing training for intercultural competence, implicit bias and equity, leadership academies, equitable hiring, and cultural inclusion.
- Faculty participation in equity efforts include areas such as planning, inclusive pedagogy, professional development, and serving on committees to promote equity efforts.
- While faculty are engaged in equity work, the level of engagement is not as high for faculty as for other stakeholder groups.
- The level of engagement in equity efforts were higher for staff than for faculty.

- Slightly over half of the institutions were examining their policies to include an equity focus.
- The data revealed that the majority of the participating institutions were in the process of implementing the process for becoming an equity-centered institution.

The unique focus of this book is to shed light on how a theoretical change model can be used to provide a methodological approach to implementing complex and sensitive initiatives such as equity. The book also provides a comparative analysis of how several community colleges report their readiness to launch equity efforts together with equity support mechanisms, which are currently in place at those institutions.

The need for comparative research on access and equity in community colleges is essential in the context of the further expansion of the completion agenda in community colleges. Our work in this book notes that attitudes and policies relating to equity as well as the consciousness among administrators is different at different institutions. Without question, community colleges will continue to be affected by inequities in their policies and practices. We believe that a systematic change model is a strategic approach to move the effort forward.

12

LAUNCH THE CALL
TO ACTION

What Does an Equity-Centered
Institution Look Like?

W e began this book by saying that it is possible for institutions to use Kotter's eight-step change model as a strategic approach to launch efforts to become an equity-centered institution. But, an equity-centered institution is hard to come by. How then can we know what an equity-centered institution looks like after the Kotter's change model steps have been followed? The purpose of this chapter is to illustrate what the equity-centered college looks like at each step in the change process.

The first step in Kotter's eight-step change model tells us that there must be a sense of urgency to propel institutions to take action. We believe that the high number of students leaving college after 4 to 5 years without a degree or a good-paying job should create a sense of urgency. (See Table 12.1.)

American community colleges educate seven million higher education students in America (AACC, 2020). With this level of enrollment, community college leaders have a responsibility to ensure equitable practices and equity-infused teaching and learning environments. Becoming an equity-centered institution requires institutions to change. To achieve this goal, an institutional transformation focused on equity and undergirded in the AACC leadership competencies (see Appendix C) is necessary. But, how do the colleges get there?

We believe that to fully take advantage of the opportunity this book presents, transformational change, it is imperative to integrate equity principles in the culture of the institution. Institutions must abandon the mind-set that leads to dead-end efforts and embrace new strategies that lead to sustainable results.

TABLE 12.1
The Equity-Centered Institution

Kotter's Transformational Change Steps	The Equity-Centered Institution
1. Create a sense of urgency: Create the catalyst for change.	Strengths, weaknesses, opportunities, and threats (SWOT) were identified to make the case for urgency. Courageous conversations and analysis of representational and achievement disparities were identified. Representational inequities in the workplace were identified. Buy-in from at least 75% of the leadership team was evident. Considerable time was spent on making the case to take action to address the urgency to do something about inequities.
2. Build a guiding coalition: Assemble a group with enough power to lead the change effort.	The institution identified and engaged a diverse group of influential employees (status, title, expertise, formal or informal power). Employees made an emotional commitment to address inequities at all levels of the institution. Team-building training was undertaken where needed. A broad range of institutional representation (different departments and status within the institution) engaged in the equity work.
3. Create a vision for change: Create a vision to help direct the change effort.	There was an examination of the mission, vision, and core values of the institution. An equity-vision statement was developed. The equity vision was linked to the existing vision and core values. Clear strategies were identified to execute the equity vision. All employees were able to articulate equity vision.

(Continues)

TABLE 12.1 (*Continued*)

Kotter's Transformational Change Steps	The Equity-Centered Institution
4. Communicate the vision: Use every channel and vehicle of communication possible to communicate the new vision and strategies.	There was continuous communication of the change in the vision among all stakeholders. There was strategic communication of the vision to all stakeholders. The equity vision was connected to performance reviews, professional development, strategic plan, etc. The concerns and issues of people were handled in an honest way. There were courageous conversations with the board of trustees to create a sense of urgency for policy development needs.
5. Remove barriers: Remove obstacles to change.	Organizational processes and structure were in place and aligned with the overall organizational vision. Organizational structures were reviewed and changed to the extent possible. Curriculum and services were reviewed and evaluated. Barriers or people who are resisting change were identified and to the extent possible were removed. Institutions took proactive actions to remove the obstacles involved in the process of change. People were rewarded for endorsing the change and supporting the process. Professional development training was conducted at all levels of the institution.
6. Create short-term wins: Recognize and reward employees involved in these improvements.	Early in the process, short-term wins were identified and celebrated. There were many short-term targets instead of one long-term goal. Contributions of people who were involved in the change process were recognized. The wins were communicated throughout the institution. Strategic communication plans were developed and messages were consistent with equity vision statement.

TABLE 12.1 (*Continued*)

Kotter's Transformational Change Steps	The Equity-Centered Institution
7. Consolidate improvements: Reinvigorate the processes with new projects, themes, and change agents.	Processes to evaluate progress were identified. Continuous improvement is ongoing. Collection and analysis of data is now part of the institutions' culture. Leaders made data-informed decisions. Policy areas within the institution that can continue to drive the transformation were identified. Resources to support equity (fiscal and human) were allocated or reallocated. CEOs and leadership team members demonstrated a strong commitment to avoid the perception of the equity work being a fad. Policies and practices reflect the commitment to equity mindedness.
8. Institute the change: Create the connections between new behaviors and corporate behaviors.	There was discussion of the successful stories related to change initiatives on every given opportunity. Equity has become an integral part of the organizational culture and is visible in every organizational aspect. The support of the existing leaders was evident. Processes to identify new leaders are now in place. Policies and practices now reflect equity principles. Equity is now incorporated into the strategic plan to send a message to the college: This work is important!

Now is the time for community college CEOs to take the bold step to make an investment in the institution and its people. Once the investment occurs, the college community is more likely to follow the equity vision. Several major areas of concern emerged from our pilot survey of institutions regarding readiness for equity:

- Faculty engagement: Leaders should consider opportunities for faculty to contribute to the development of the equity agenda and their daily engagement with students and one another. If faculty are not a part of the conversation, it will be difficult to bring them along. Using the leadership competency of effective communication will guide these conversations.
- Teaching and learning: The department/division chairs and deans should utilize the leadership competency of collaboration with and through the faculty to develop curriculum, learning outcomes, and assessment plans that include equity.
- Student engagement: The EOT will need to meet with student leaders to determine the best approaches to engage students. In a community college setting, these strategies rest largely on timing since we have such a transient population. Consider clubs and their constitutions or bylaws—do they include the principles of equity?
- Staff engagement: Similar to the faculty, change will be hard with this group without the leadership competencies of communication and collaboration. Ensure that employees are connected and see the WIFM (what's in it for me) effect.
- Professional development: Invest in leadership development using the AACC leadership competencies as a guide. As Maxwell (2011) opines in his book *The Five Levels of Leadership*, true leaders invest in others.
- Policy and practices: Conduct an audit of institutional policies and practices to determine if there are barriers that block equity efforts.

Ready to Get Started?

We encourage institutions to utilize the model highlighted in this text to guide equity transformation. Community college leaders must strive to maintain the efforts through becoming skilled at putting best practices into place to improve equity outcomes. Take the first step by launching a conversation with institutional leaders around the ideas presented in this book.

REFERENCES

Achieving the Dream. (n.d.a). *About us.* https://www.achievingthedream.org/about-us

Achieving the Dream. (n.d.b). *Our approach.* https://www.achievingthedream.org/our-network/our-approach

Achieving the Dream. (n.d.c). *Achieving the Dream equity statement.* https://www.achievingthedream.org/focus-areas/equity

Achieving the Dream. (n.d.d). *Holistic student support services.* https://www.achievingthedream.org/our-services/holistic-student-supports-redesign-coaching-program

Achieving the Dream. (2018a, October 4). *Holistic student supports redesign toolkit.* https://www.achievingthedream.org/resource/17502/holistic-student-supports-redesign-a-toolkit

Achieving the Dream. (2018b, October 8). *Implementing a holistic student supports approach: Four case studies.* https://www.achievingthedream.org/resource/17504/implementing-a-holistic-student-supports-approach-four-case-studies

Alfred, R., Shults, C., Jaquette, O. & Strickland, S. (2009). *Community colleges on the horizon: Challenge, choice, or abundance.* Rowman & Littlefield Education.

American Association of Community Colleges. (2018). *AACC competencies for community college leaders.* https://www.aacc.nche.edu/wp-content/uploads/2018/11/AACC2018Competencies_111618_FINAL.pdf

American Association of Community Colleges. (2020). *Fast facts.* https://www.aacc.nche.edu/research-trends/fast-facts/

Anicich, E. M. & Hirsh, J. B. (2017a). The psychology of middle power: Vertical code-switching, role conflict, and behavioral inhibition. *Academy of Management Review, 42*(4), 659–682.

Anicich, E. M. & Hirsh, J. B. (2017b, March 22). Why being a middle manager is so exhausting. *Harvard Business Review.* https://hbr.org/2017/03/why-being-a-middle-manager-is-so-exhausting

Bailey, T. R., Jaggars, S. S., & Jenkins, D. (2015). *Redesigning America's community colleges: A clearer path to student success.* Harvard University Press.

Beatty, K. (2011). *Empowering Black women to lead: A phenomenological study examining the role of the NCBAA institute in the development of midlevel community college administrators* [Doctoral dissertation, Morgan State University, Baltimore, Maryland].

Bensimon, E. M. (2005). Equality as a fact, equality as a result: A matter of institutional accountability (Commissioned Paper). Washington DC: American Council on Education.

Bryan-Gooden, J. M., Hester, & L. Q. Peoples. (2019). *Culturally responsive curriculum scorecard.* Metropolitan Center for Research on Equity and the Transformation of Schools, New York University.

Burke, W. W. (2008). *Foundations for organizational science. Organization change: Theory and practice* (2nd ed.). Sage.

Center for Urban Education. (2018). *Equity minded inquiry series: Syllabus review.* Series presented at the Rossier School of Education, University of Southern California, Los Angeles, CA.

Cohen, A. M., Brawer, F. B., & Kisker, C. B. (2014). *The American community college* (6th ed.). Jossey Bass.

Colorado Community College System. (2020, June 25). *Equity and Inclusion Council.* https://internal.cccs.edu/student-affairs/councils-committees-taskforces/equity-and-inclusion-council/

Covey, S. R. (2006). *The SPEED of trust: The one thing that changes everything.* Simon and Schuster.

Evans, R. (1996). *The human side of school change: Reform, resistance, and the real-life problems of innovation.* Jossey-Bass.

Ewell, P. T. (2010). *Data collection and use at community colleges.* White House Summit on Community Colleges. http://www. ed.gov/college-completion/community-college-summit

Feagin, J. R. (2006). *Systemic racism: A theory of oppression.* Routledge.

Floyd, S. W., & Wooldridge, B. (1992). Middle management involvement in strategy and its association with strategic type: A research note. *Strategic Management Journal, 13,* 153–167. https://www.jstor.org/stable/2486358

Gray, J. (2019, May 30). *What students see that we don't: Students are noticing, noticing if we notice, and noticing we do.* Paper presented at Achieving the Dream 2019 Teaching and Learning Summit, Minneapolis, MN.

Johnson, J. A. (2014). The ethics of big data in higher education. *International Review of Information Ethics, 7*(18), 3–10. http://www.i-r-i-e.net/inhalt/021/IRIE-021-Johnson.pdf?imm_mid=0c8f35&cmp=em-data-na-na-newsltr_20141217

Jones, C. (2019, May 17). NJC first college in Colorado Community College System to sign equity and inclusion pledge. *Journal-Advocate.* https://www.journal-advocate.com/2019/04/18/njc-first-college-in-colorado-community-college-system-to-sign-equity-and-inclusion-pledge/

Kim, W. C., & Mauborngne, R. (2005). *Blue ocean strategy.* Harvard Business School Press.

Kotter, J. P. (1996). *Leading change.* Harvard Business School Press.

Kotter, J. P. (2014). *Accelerate: Building strategic agility for a faster-moving world.* Harvard Business School Press.

Maxwell, J. C. (2007). *The 21 irrefutable laws of leadership: Follow them and people will follow you.* Thomas Nelson.

Maxwell, J. C. (2011). *5 levels of leadership: Proven steps to maximize your potential.* Center Street.

Maxwell, J. P. (2004). *Today matters.* Warner Books.

McChesney, C., Covey, S., & Huling, J. (2012). *The 4 disciplines of execution: Achieving your wildly important goals.* Simon & Schuster.

McClenney, K. (2016, September). *Strengthening student success* [Keynote address]. TYFY Conference, Denver, Colorado.

McPhail, C. J. (2016). From tall to matrix: Redefining organizational structures. *Change: The Magazine of Higher Learning, 48*(4), 55–62. https://doi.org/10.1080/00091383.2016.1198189

Moore, W. (2006). *Behind the open door: Racism and other contradictions in the community college.* Trafford.

New England Resource Center for Higher Education. (2019). *NERCHE self-assessment rubric for the institutionalization of diversity, equity, and inclusion in higher education.* https://www.wpi.edu/sites/default/files/Project_Inclusion_NERCHE_Rubric-Self-Assessment-2016.pdf

O'Banion, T. (2011). Pathways to completion: Guidelines to boosting student success. *Community College Journal, 82*(1), 28–34. http://www.ccjournal-digital.com/ccjournal/20110809?search_term=Pathways%20to%20Completion&doc_id=-1&search_term=Pathways%20to%20Completion&pg=30#pg30

Rowley, D. J., Lujan, H. D., & Dolence, M. G. (1997). *Strategic change in colleges and universities: Planning to survive and prosper.* Jossey-Bass.

Slaughter, J. (2003). *The search for excellence in higher education. A perspective from an engineer.* Unpublished paper presented at the Woodruff Distinguished Lecture, The George W. Woodruff School of Mechanical Engineering, Georgia Institute of Technology, Atlanta, Georgia.

Institutional Self-Assessment for Equity

Dimension I: Philosophy and Mission of Equity—A feature of an institutionalized equity effort is the development of a shared definition for equity that provides meaning, focus, and emphasis for institutional renewal and transformation. The definition of equity and how broadly that definition is understood will determine the degree to which constituents participate, the level of financial support toward equity, and the degree to which equity becomes integrated into the campus culture.

1. Please indicate your level of agreement for each of the following statements.
My institution has a(an):

	Strongly Agree	Agree	Neither Agree nor Disagree	Disagree	Strongly Disagree
definition of equity.	◯	◯	◯	◯	◯
strategic plan with an equity focus.	◯	◯	◯	◯	◯
institution mission including equity.	◯	◯	◯	◯	◯
initiatives or transformation efforts including equity.	◯	◯	◯	◯	◯
accreditation process including equity as a factor.	◯	◯	◯	◯	◯
institutional history which includes elements of equity.	◯	◯	◯	◯	◯

2. **Please include evidence that supports your perspective of Dimension I.** Indicators should be tangible, for example, equity programming, a specific professional development opportunity, or other factors that contribute to the equity agenda.

Transformational Change: Becoming an Equity-Centered Higher Education Institution Assessment

Dimension II: Faculty Support for and involvement in Equity—An important element for equity institutionalization is the degree to which the faculty take ownership of equity as essential to the academic core of the institution

3. Please indicate your level of agreement for each of the following statements.

At my institution, <u>Faculty</u>:

	Strongly Agree	Agree	Neither Agree nor Disagree	Disagree	Strongly Disagree
have knowledge and awareness of equity.	◯	◯	◯	◯	◯
are involved and support equity.	◯	◯	◯	◯	◯
demonstrate leadership efforts to advance equity.	◯	◯	◯	◯	◯
are rewarded for engagement in equity efforts.	◯	◯	◯	◯	◯
have incentives for development of equity engagement.	◯	◯	◯	◯	◯
have academic departments that infuse equity into academic programs.	◯	◯	◯	◯	◯

4. **Please include evidence that supports your perspective of Dimension II.**Indicators should be tangible, for example, equity programming, a specific professional development opportunity, or other factors that contribute to the equity agenda.

Dimension III: Teaching, Research, and Service Supporting Equity —One of the essential factors for institutionalizing equity in community colleges is the degree to which faculty are involved in the implementation and advancement of pedagogy, research, scholarship and services related to equity.

5. Please indicate your level of agreement for each of the following statements.

At my institution, <u>Faculty</u>:

	Strongly Agree	Agree	Neither Agree nor Disagree	Disagree	Strongly Disagree
have knowledge and awareness of equity in relation to disciplines.	○	○	○	○	○
develop curriculum with an equity focus.	○	○	○	○	○
incorporate equity in teaching and learning strategies and methods.	○	○	○	○	○
use teaching and learning resources that incorporate equity.	○	○	○	○	○
have student learning outcomes focused on equity.	○	○	○	○	○
engage in research that incorporates equity.	○	○	○	○	○

6. **Please include evidence that supports your perspective of Dimension III.** Indicators should be tangible, for example, equity programming, a specific professional development opportunity, or other factors that contribute to the equity agenda.

Transformational Change: Becoming an Equity-Centered Higher Education
Institution Assessment

Dimension IV: Staff Engagement and Involvement in Equity —One of the essential factors for institutionalizing equity in higher education is the degree to which staff members are involved in the implementation and advancement of equity.

7. Please indicate your level of agreement for each of the following statements.
At my institution, Staff:

	Strongly Agree	Agree	Neither Agree nor Disagree	Disagree	Strongly Disagree
have knowledge and awareness of equity.	○	○	○	○	○
are involved and support equity.	○	○	○	○	○
demonstrate leadership efforts to advance equity.	○	○	○	○	○
are rewarded for engagement in equity efforts.	○	○	○	○	○
have incentives for the development of equity engagement.	○	○	○	○	○
have support services that infuse equity into academic programs.	○	○	○	○	○

8. **Please include evidence that supports your perspective of Dimension IV.** Indicators should be tangible, for example, equity programming, a specific professional development opportunity, or other factors that contribute to the equity agenda.

Transformational Change: Becoming an Equity-Centered Higher Education
Institution Assessment

Dimension V: Student Support for and Involvement in Equity —An important element of equity institutionalization is the degree to which students are provided the opportunities to learn about equity in co-curricular settings; are aware of these opportunities; engaged in these opportunities; and plan a leadership role in the development of diversity on campus.

9. Please indicate your level of agreement for each of the following statements.
At my institution, <u>Student(s)</u>:

	Strongly Agree	Agree	Neither Agree nor Disagree	Disagree	Strongly Disagree
have knowledge and awareness of equity.	○	○	○	○	○
have success metrics linked to equity.	○	○	○	○	○
are involved and support equity.	○	○	○	○	○
demonstrate leadership efforts to advance equity.	○	○	○	○	○
are rewarded for engagement in equity efforts.	○	○	○	○	○

10. **Please include evidence that supports your perspective of Dimension V.**Indicators should be tangible, for example, equity programming, a specific professional development opportunity, or other factors that contribute to the equity agenda.

Dimension VI: Administrative Leadership and Institutional Support for Equity —In or for equity to become institutionalized on community college campuses, senior leadership must demonstrate commitment and ensure that the institution provides substantial resources, support, and accountability toward the effort.

11. Please indicate your level of agreement for each of the following statements.
At my institution, <u>Administrative Leadership</u>:

	Strongly Agree	Agree	Neither Agree nor Disagree	Disagree	Strongly Disagree
support the coordination of equity efforts.	○	○	○	○	○
develop policy that includes equity.	○	○	○	○	○
has a designated position to support and coordinate equity efforts.	○	○	○	○	○
has hiring and retention efforts that support equity.	○	○	○	○	○
has professional development that includes equity.	○	○	○	○	○
allocates funding to support equity.	○	○	○	○	○
have knowledge and awareness of equity.	○	○	○	○	○
utilizes/tracks institutional research data with an equity focus.	○	○	○	○	○

12. **Please include evidence that supports your perspective of Dimension VI.**Indicators should be tangible, for example, equity programming, a specific professional development opportunity, or other factors that contribute to the equity agenda.

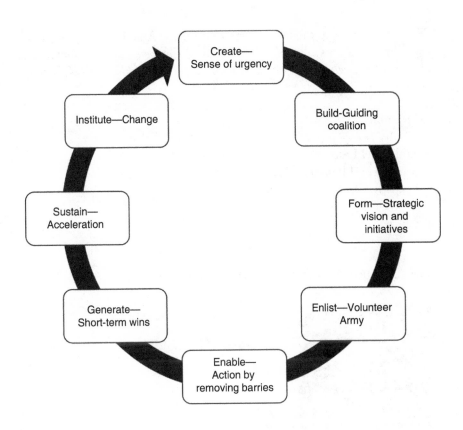

AACC Leadership Competencies

The following is the table of contents for the American Association of Community Colleges's (2018) *AACC Competencies for Community College Leaders.* You can view the full PDF by scanning the QR code in Figure C.1.

Preamble   3
Faculty   7
Mid-Level Leaders   21
Senior-Level Leaders 35
Aspiring CEOs   49
New CEOs   63
CEOs   77

Figure C.1. QR code for *AACC Competencies for Community College Leaders.*

Source: American Association of Community Colleges (2018).
https://www.aacc.nche.edu/wp-content/uploads/2018/11/AACC2018Competencies_111618_FINAL.pdf

ABOUT THE AUTHORS

Christine Johnson McPhail is president at Saint Augustine's University in Raleigh, NC. She is a nationally recognized thought leader in higher education. McPhail is the founding professor and director of the Community College Leadership Doctoral Program at Morgan State University. She formerly served as president of Cypress College in California. She is a certified associate for Emergenetics International, which helps organizations, ranging from small businesses to Fortune 500 companies, achieve desired results including increased efficiency and improved communication through solutions centered on the Emergenetics Profile and tools. She is the editor for one of AACC's best-selling publications, *Establishing and Sustaining Learning-Centered Community Colleges*, the coauthor of the best-selling *Practical Leadership in Community Colleges* with George Boggs, and the author of *Leadership Tune-Up: Twelve Steps to Becoming a More Successful and Innovative Leader*. McPhail was the recipient of the 2018 Diverse Champions Award. The Diverse Champions Award recognizes higher education leaders who have shown unwavering commitment to equal opportunity and access for all, particularly at the community college level.

Kimberly Beatty, EdD, began her tenure as Metropolitan Community College's eighth chancellor on July 1, 2017. She was formally installed as chancellor at an inauguration ceremony on August. 24, 2018. Beatty came to MCC from Houston Community College, the nation's fourth-largest community college system, where she served as vice chancellor for instructional services and chief academic officer. As the first African-American leader in the 105-year history of Metropolitan Community College, and the only African-American CEO in the Missouri community college system, "I live and walk in the truth of who I am each day," Beatty says. A champion of access and equity, she is devoted to the community college mission of providing access to higher education for all. "I am passionate about the community I serve and excited about the ability to provide higher education access to the underprivileged and underrepresented," Beatty says.

AACC. *See* American Association of Community College
access, to education, 6–7
accountability, 60, 61–62, 76–77, 81
accountability system, 59, 61
achievement disparities, 2, 47
  students of color and, 15–16
achievement gaps, 64, 76
Achieving the Dream (ATD), 17, 37–38, 88–89
  coaching and, 91–92, 93
  equity statement for, 90–92, 95
  teaching and learning and, 93–94
active listening, 35, 40, 44
  communicating equity vision and, 45
administrative leadership, 21, 23, 106, 110, 112
administrative review, 19
administrators, 46, 50–51
advocacy, 9
  leadership and, 39
advocacy behavior, 33
agenda. *See* equity agenda
American Association of Community College's (AACC) leadership competencies, ix, xi–xii, 32, 114
  EOT and, 28–29
  overview of, 9–10
analysis, of data collection, 35–36
analytics, AACC competency, 9
army, volunteer, 12
assessment, curriculum, 94. *See also* institutional equity assessment
ATD. *See* Achieving the Dream

bargaining units, 84
barrier removal management, 61–62

barriers, 61, 94. *See also* equity barriers
  communication, 66–67
  structural, 60
barriers and leadership competency matrix, 61
Beatty, Kimberly, 73–74, 98–99
behavior
  advocacy, 33
  principles aligned with, 30–31
Bensimon, E. M., 3, 6
"big impact," identifying, 35–36
Black students, 2, 89, 98
board, of trustees, 46, 51–52
broad-based engagement, 19
building, team, 32–36, 59
  visioning session for, 39
burn out, 75
buy-in, from stakeholders, 29, 31

CAO. *See* chief academic officer
capacity, for change, 72–74
CCCS. *See* Colorado Community College Systems
CCSSE. *See* community college survey of student engagement
CDI. *See* Center for Diversity and Innovation
celebration, of short-term wins, 69–70
Center for Diversity and Innovation (CDI), 96–97
"CEO Action Pledge for Diversity and Inclusion" (The Pledge), 101
CEOs, 16–17, 58, 67–68, 74, 117
  vision and, 38
challenges, 58. *See also* equity challenges
  with institutional culture, 83–85

champion, leader, 24–25, 32, 47–48
change, 8, 83. *See also* Kotter's
  eight-stage change model
  capacity for, 72–74
  hiring procedure, 66
  "lid" for, 74
  lifestyle, 73
  need for, 44–45
  outcomes of, 78–81
  plateau stage of, 73–74
  resistance to, 4, 56, 66, 71–72
  stages of, xii, 73–74
  urgency for, 13–15, 24
change process, x, 11, 13, 17, 86, 114.
  See also Kotter's eight-stage
  change model
  organizational culture and, 57
chief academic officer (CAO), 74
climate survey, 97
coaching, ATD, 91–92, 93
coalition. *See* equity oversight team
  (EOT)
collaboration, AACC competency, 9,
  11–12
College Resources for Advanced Faculty
  Training (CRAFT), 93
Colorado Community College Systems
  (CCCS), 88, 99–103
Columbus State Community College,
  93
committees
  executive, 49
  hiring, 31
common goals, for EOT, 33, 39
  strategies for, 34–36
communication, 42, 97
  AACC competency, 9, 11, 35
  goals of, 45
  of short-term wins, 68–69
communication barriers, 66–67
communication plan, for equity vision,
  43–44, 55, 65
  Phase 1 for, 45–53
  Phase 2 for, 53
  Phase 3 for, 53–54

Community College Leadership
  Program, University of Texas at
  Austin, 2
community college reform initiatives, 1
community college scholars, ix
community college survey of student
  engagement (CCSSE), 24, 34, 53
competencies. *See* American Association
  of Community College's (AACC)
  leadership competencies
competition, equity, 80–81
complacency, 15
components, of institutional equity
  assessment, 22–23
conflict management, 31
consultants, 36
conversations, 95
  equity, 2, 6, 20, 31
  reset, 84–85
core values, xi, 4
councils, diversity and inclusion, 99
Covey, Sean, 11, 78
CRAFT (College Resources for
  Advanced Faculty Training), 93
create trust, for EOT, 30–32
cultivation, relationship, 12, 75
cultural competence educational
  opportunities, 3
culture, 84–85
  equity and, 56, 72
  institutional, 15, 21, 32, 82–83
  organizational, 9, 11, 15
  power of, 85–86
curriculum, on equity, 22
curriculum assessment, 94

data collection, 17, 113
  analysis of, 35–36
  for common goals, 34–35
  for institutional equity assessment,
    23–24, 90, 105–7
  sense-of-urgency and, 25–26, 50
data teams, 34–35
deconstruction of equity, 100

"democracy's colleges," ix
development, professional, 24, 33, 93, 108–9, 112, 118
DIALED campaign (Diversity, Inclusion, Achievement, Learning, Exploration of Data, and the Deconstruction of Equity), 100
dilemmas, ethical, 67
dimensions, for institutional equity assessment, 19–21, 105–6, 107–10
director, of equity and inclusion, 98–99
discrimination, 2, 57, 91
discussion groups, with stakeholders, 47–53
disparities
  achievement, 2, 15–16, 47
  educational, 2
  equity, 1, 90
diversity, 19
  embracing, 15
  of faculty, 64–65, 66
Diversity, Inclusion, Achievement, Learning, Exploration of Data, and the Deconstruction of Equity (DIALED campaign), 100
diversity and inclusion councils, 99

education, access to, 6–7
EIC. See Equity and Inclusion Committee
electronic newsletters, 65
embracing diversity, 15
employee engagement, 30
employee satisfaction survey, 24
engagement
  broad-based, 19
  employee, 30
  faculty, 106, 107, 109, 112, 118
  staff, 21, 22, 106, 109–10, 118
  of stakeholders, 18–19, 57, 102
  student, 118
engagement plan, 48, 49, 50, 51, 52
enrollment systems, 57

EOT. See equity oversight team
equality
  equity and, 6, 7
  racial, 6
equitable outcomes, ix
equity, ix, xi, xii–xiii, 1–13, 15, 19. See also Institutional Equity Assessment
  culture and, 56, 72
  curriculum on, 22
  equality and, 6, 7
  goals for, 22
  integration of, 21
  partnerships for, 75–76
  philosophy of, 20, 21, 22
  representational, 6
  resistance to, 38, 98
  resource, 6, 18
equity agenda, x, 3–4, 16. See also specific topics
  EOT and, 36
  stakeholders embracing, 30, 31
equity and inclusion, director of, 98–99
Equity and Inclusion Committee (EIC), 96, 97, 98, 100–101
equity and inclusion officer, 98
equity barriers, 55–56
  EOT and, 57–58
  institutional leadership and, 58
  as lid, 58
  removing, 58–62
  systemic, 57
equity capacity-building process, 97
equity-centered institutions, xi, 65, 115–17
  framework for, 10–13, 14
  goals for, 34
  inquiry for, 17
  trust and, 30
  vision for, 37–41
equity-centeredness, 2–3
equity challenges
  leading, 5–8
  sense-of-urgency and, 15–16
equity competition, 80–81

equity conversations, 2, 6, 20, 31
equity disparities, 1, 90
equity efforts, study on, 105
equity impact, 29
"equity institute," 75
equity lens, 6–8
equity-mindedness, 3, 6, 8, 10
equity-oriented phrases, 72
equity oversight team (EOT), 27, 51,
    53, 71–72
  common goals for, 33–36
  equity agenda and, 36
  equity barriers and, 57–58
  institutional leadership used by,
    83–84
  leadership competencies for, 28–29
  right people for, 29
  senior leaders and, 28–29, 33
  transparency and, 31–32
  trust created for, 30–32
  vision and, 39–41, 43, 46
Equity Road Tour, 102
equity rubric, 20, 23. *See also*
    Institutional Equity Assessment
equity statement, for ATD, 90–92, 95
equity training models, 59
equity vision, 39–41, 42, 74. *See also*
    communication plan, for equity
    vision
  communication of, 43–45
  communication plan for, 45–54
  stakeholders and, 46–47, 78
  strategies for, 80–81
equity vision statement, 41, 54, 99
ethical dilemmas, 67
evaluation process, 60, 76–77
Everett Community College, 91
examination, self-, 66
executive committees, 49
executive leadership team, 47–48

faculty, 25, 46, 48–49, 94–95
  diversity of, 64–65, 66
  leaders and, 72

faculty engagement, 106, 107, 109,
    112, 118
faculty support, 21, 22
fairness, 7
The Five Levels of Leadership
    (Maxwell), 118
followership, 63, 67, 79
forums
  for communicating equity vision, 47
  information, 75
  student, 52–53
The 4 Disciplines of Execution
    (McChesney, Covey, Huling),
    78, 81
framework, for equity-centered
    institutions, 10–13, 14
fundraising, 9, 75–76

gaps, achievement, 64, 76
Garcia, Joe, 100
Giese, Melissa, 105
give-and-take strategy, 53
goals
  of communication, 45
  EOT common, 33–36, 39
  for equity, 22
  for equity-centered institutions, 34
  performance, 76–77
  relevance, xi–xii
  short-term wins and, 68–70
  stakeholders and, 33
goal-setting sessions, 34
governance, 9, 11, 12–13, 24
  leadership and, 25, 43–44
governance leaders, 29, 43–44
governance structure, 25, 45–53, 76, 84
grants, Pell, 92
growth, personal, 67
guiding coalition. *see* equity oversight
    team (EOT)

hiring committee, 31
hiring procedure changes, 66

Hispanic students, 2
holistic support, 92–93
Huling, Jim, 78

ICAT. *See* institutional capacity
    assessment tool
impact, equity, 29
implicit bias training, 97
incentives, 107
    for students, 52, 112
inclusion, 3, 19, 96–101
inclusive pedagogy, 109, 112
indicators, for institutional equity
    assessment, 23
influence, and leadership, 63
information forum, 75
infrastructure, institutional, 9, 12
inquiry, equity-centered, 17
institutional capacity assessment tool
    (ICAT), 90
institutional culture, 15, 21, 32, 82
    challenges with, 83–85
institutional equity assessment, 18
    components of, 22–23
    data collection for, 23–24, 90, 105–7
    dimensions of, 19–21, 105–6,
        107–10
    indicators for, 23
    key findings for, 112–13
    protocol for, 19
    survey for, 105–13, 123–29
institutional infrastructure, 9, 12
institutional leadership, 9, 12, 28, 44,
    61, 78
    EOT using, 83–84
    equity barriers and, 58
institutional perspectives, 95–103
institutional readiness, 16–17, 18,
    117–18
    stages of, 23, 111–13
Institutional Research Office, 17–18,
    24, 70
institutions, 108–9. *See also* equity-
    centered institutions

types of, 107, 111, 112
integration
    of equity, 21
    of short-term wins, 68–70

Kellogg Community College (KCC),
    88, 95–98
Kotter's eight-stage change model, ix,
    xii, 14, 78, 114–17, 130
    overview of, 8
Kotter's "guiding coalition" concept, 27
Kotter's sense-of-urgency approach,
    14–15, 26. *See also* sense-of-
    urgency

leaders
    champion, 24–25, 32
    faculty and, 72
    governance, 29, 43–44
    senior, 25, 28–29, 32, 34, 81
leadership, xii, 4, 11, 16–17, 44,
    60–61, 79. *See also* American
    Association of Community
    College's (AACC) leadership
    competencies
    administrative, 21, 23, 106, 110, 112
    advocacy and, 39
    governance and, 25
    influence and, 63
    institutional, 9, 12, 28, 78
    organization and, 5
    role of, 68
    trust and, 30
leadership development institutes, 72
leadership team, 5
    executive, 47–48
    senior, 8, 19, 80
leading change, xii
leading equity challenge, 5–8
learning. *See* teaching and learning
legislation, state level, 77
lens, equity, 6–8
"lid"

for change, 74
  equity barriers as, 58
lifestyle changes, 73
listening, active, 35, 40, 44
low-income students, 88, 90

management
  barrier removal, 61–62
  role of, 68
managers, midlevel, 25, 51, 67, 72
Maxwell, J. C., 118
MCC. *See* Metropolitan Community
  College
McChesney, Chris, 78
McClenney, Kay, 52
metaphors
  potato, 79–80
  spider web, 78
  weight loss, 73
Metropolitan Community College
  (MCC), 88, 98–99
midlevel managers, 25, 51, 67, 72
misunderstandings, 72
mobilization, stakeholder, 33
Moore, Bill, 2
morale, 73

national perspectives, 88
New England Resource Center for
  Higher Education (NERCHE),
  18–19
newsletters, electronic, 65
"next steps," 48, 49, 50, 51, 95
North Arkansas College, 92
Northeastern Junior College, 101

O'Banion, Terry, 56
observation, student, 94
obstacles, 87
officer, equity and inclusion, 98
open-door admission policies, 2
opportunities, cultural competence
  educational, 3

organization, and leadership, 5
organizational culture, 9, 11, 15
  change process and, 57
organizational structures, 56–57
outcomes, of change, 78–81

partnerships, for equity, 75–76
"Pathways to Completion"
  (O'Banion), 56
pedagogy, ix, 21, 22, 25, 106
  inclusive, 109, 112
Pell grants, 92
performance goals, 76–77
performance management system,
  59, 76
personal growth, 67
perspectives
  institutional, 95–103
  national, 88
phases of communication, of equity
  vision, 45–54
philosophy, of equity, 20, 21, 22
phrases, equity-oriented, 72
Pirius, Landon, 100
plan, engagement, 48, 49, 50, 51, 52
plateau stage, of change, 73–74
The Pledge ("CEO Action Pledge for
  Diversity and Inclusion"), 101
policies, 76
  open-door admission, 2
potato metaphor, 79–80
poverty, systemic, 94
power, of culture, 85–86
practical application goal, xii
principles, behavior aligned with,
  30–31
problem-solving techniques, 31
process. *See also* change process
  equity capacity-building, 97
  evaluation, 60, 76–77
professional development, 24, 33, 93,
  108–9, 112, 118
Protocol, for institutional Equity
  Assessment, 19

quality, of experience, 16

race, 3, 83
racial equality, 6
racial tensions, 1–2
racism, 89, 91, 94
 systemic, 57
readiness
 for equity, 117–18
 institutional, 16–17, 18, 23, 111–13,
 117–18
reform initiatives, community college, 1
relationship cultivation, 12, 75
relevance goal, xi–xii
removal, of equity barriers, 58–62
representational equity, 6
reset conversations, 84–85
resistance
 to change, 4, 56, 66, 71–72
 to equity, 38, 97
resource equity, 6, 18
retreats, for team building, 32
review, administrative, 19
revision, syllabi, 94
right people, for EOT, 29
rubric, equity, 20, 23. *See also*
 Institutional Equity Assessment
Ryan, Ross, 99–103

scholars, community college, ix
self-assessment rubric, NERCHE,
 18, 19
self-examination, 66
senior leaders, 25, 32, 81
 EOT and, 28–29, 34
senior leadership team, 8, 19, 80
SENSE. *See* survey of entering student
 engagement
sense-of-urgency, 13, 24, 27, 49, 52
 data collection and, 25–26, 50
 equity challenges and, 15–16
 Kotter's, 14–15, 26
 readiness for equity and, 16–17

short-term wins and, 64
 statement for, 48
shared vision, 48, 49, 50, 51, 53
short-term wins, 63, 71
 celebrating, 69–70
 communication of, 68–69
 goals and, 68–70
 integration of, 68–70
 planning for, 67–68
 role of, 65–67
 sense-of-urgency and, 64
 transparency of, 64
Slaughter, John Brooks, 2
social media, 65
The SPEED of Trust (Covey), 11
spider web metaphor, 78
staff, 46, 49–50
staff engagement, 21, 22, 106,
 109–10, 118
stages
 of change, xii, 73–74
 of institutional readiness, 23,
 111–13
stakeholder mobilization, 33
stakeholders, 3, 8, 11–12, 65, 79
 buy-in from, 29, 31
 discussion groups with, 47–53
 engagement of, 18–19, 57, 102
 equity agenda embraced by, 30, 31
 equity vision and, 46–47, 78
 goals and, 33
state level legislation, 77
statements. *See also* equity statement,
 for ATD
 equity vision, 41, 54
 sense-of-urgency, 48
 vision, 37–38, 40, 52, 54, 66
Stout, Karen, 38, 88
strategic plan, college, 4
strategies, xii–xiii
 for EOT common goals, 34–36
 for equity vision, 80–81
 give-and-take, 53
structural barriers, 60

structure, governance, 25, 45–53, 76, 84
structures, organizational, 56
student engagement, 118
student forums, 52–53
student observation, 94
students, 21, 46, 53, 106, 110
  Black, 2, 89, 98
  Hispanic, 2
  holistic support for, 92–93
  incentives for, 52, 112
  low-income, 88, 90
students of color, 1, 90
  achievement disparities and, 15–16
student success, AACC competency, 9
student support, 22–23
study, on equity efforts, 105
success, student, 9
support
  faculty, 21, 22
  holistic, 92–93
  student, 22–23
survey of entering student engagement
  (SENSE), 24, 34
surveys
  CCSSE, 24
  climate, 97
  employee satisfaction, 24
  for institutional equity assessment,
    105–13, 123–29
  SENSE, 24, 34
syllabi revision, 94
systemic equity barriers, 57
systemic poverty, 94
systemic racism, 57
systems
  accountability, 59, 61
  enrollment, 57
  performance management, 59, 76

teaching and learning, 106, 109, 118
  ADT and, 93–94
team building, 32–36, 59
  visioning session for, 39
teams, data, 34–35

teamwork, 59
tensions, racial, 1–2
training, 33
  equity, 59
  implicit bias, 97
transparency, 12
  EOT and, 31–32
  of short-term equity wins, 64
trust
  created for EOT, 30–32
  equity-centered institutions and, 30
  leadership and, 30
trustees, board of, 46, 51–52

unequitable practices, identifying, 31
University of Texas at Austin, 2
urgency, for change, 13–15, 24. *See also*
  sense-of-urgency

values, core, xi, 4
vision. *See also* equity vision
  CEOs and, 38
  EOT and, 39–41, 43, 46
  for equity-centered institution,
    37–41
  shared, 48, 49, 50, 51, 53
visioning session, 39
vision statements, 37–38, 40, 52, 66
  equity, 41, 54, 99
volunteer army, 12

Washington, Jamie, 96
weight loss metaphor, 73
what's in it for me? (WIFM), 49–50,
  118
White Men and Allies (WMAA), 96
WIFM (what's in it for me?), 49–50,
  118
wins. *See* short-term wins
WMAA. *See* White Men and Allies

Zeballos, Jorge, 95–98